LIVING
through
HISTORY

the Making of the United Kingdom

Nigel Kelly, Rosemary Rees
and Jane Shuter

Heinemann

First published in Great Britain by Heinemann Library, Halley Court, Jordan Hill, Oxford OX2 8EJ, a division of Reed Educational and Professional Publishing Ltd.

OXFORD MELBOURNE AUCKLAND
JOHANNESBURG BLANTYRE GABORONE
IBADAN PORTSMOUTH (NH) USA CHICAGO

Heinemann is a registered trademark of Reed Educational and Professional Publishing Ltd.

First published 1998

01 00 99
10 9 8 7 6 5 4 3 2

British Library Cataloguing in Publication data
Kelly, Nigel, 1954-
    Living through history : the making of the United Kingdom
    1.Great Britain - History - Juvenile literature
    I.Title II.Rees, Rosemary, 1942- III.Shuter, Jane
    941

ISBN 0 431 06853 4 hardback
ISBN 0 431 06852 6 paperback

Designed and produced by Dennis Fairey and Associates Ltd.
Cover design by Wooden Ark
Printed and bound in Spain by Mateu Cromo

Illustrated by John James, Arthur Phillips, and Stephen Wisdom.

Special thanks to the Hengrave Hall Community for their enthusiastic assistance. Educational R.E. and History Days for Schools are provided by the Community in the Tudor Hall throughout the year. For further information contact: Schools Project Organiser, Hengrave Hall Centre, Bury St Edmunds, IP28 6LZ, or telephone 01284 701561.

Photographic acknowledgements

The authors and publisher would like to thank the following for permission to reproduce photographs:

Cover photograph: AKG/Erich Lessing

Blair Castle Collection, Perthshire: 4.2A
Bridgeman Art Library: 1.1B, 2.2C, D, 5.2B, 5.4C, 5.9E, p. 87, 7.3A, 7.4B, E
Bridgeman Art Library/British Library: 6.2C
Bridgeman Art Library/Museum of London: 7.5A
Bridgeman Art Library/Scottish National Portrait Gallery: 6.2B
British Library: 5.6A
British Museum: 4.3B
Cambridge University Library, Rare Books Division: 7.5B
Master and Fellows, Corpus Christi College, Oxford: 3.6A
ET Archive/Kobal Collection: 3.2A
Mary Evans Picture Library: 4.3A, 5.9B, 7.1A, E
Fotomas Index: 1.3D, 1.6C, 3.3B, 4.2C, 5.2C
Friends of Burford Church: 5.7A, B
Robert Harding Picture Library: 7.3E
Hengrave Hall Centre: 1.2B, 1.8A, B, G, 3.3A, 3.4C
House of Commons Education Unit: 2.1A
Hulton Deutsch Collection: 5.5B
Hulton-Getty Picture Collection Library: 1.6B
The Earl of Leicester and Trustees of the Holkham Estate, Norfolk: 3.1A
Mansell Collection/Time Inc.: 6.1B
Methuen Collection: 2.2E
Trustees of the National Gallery: 1.5B
National Portrait Gallery, London: 1.1C, 1.3A, p. 37, 3.6C, 5.9A
National Trust Photographic Library: 1.4A, 1.7B
Lord Petre, Ingatestone Hall, Essex: 2.1E
Pinacoteca Nazionale, Sienna: 2.2B
The Royal Collection © Her Majesty the Queen: 2.1B, 2.2A. 5.1A
Trustees of the Tate Gallery, London: 1.8F
Victoria and Albert Museum Picture Library, London: 5.8A

CONTENTS

Tudors and Stuarts

In 1485 Henry Tudor defeated King Richard III at the Battle of Bosworth and became England's first Tudor monarch. When his grand-daughter Elizabeth died in 1603 she was **succeeded** by her cousin James Stuart. From then until 1714 England was ruled by members of the Stuart family.

Henry VII was the only English monarch in this period who had to win battles to establish himself in power, but that does not mean that the other monarchs had it easy. During the sixteenth century Parliament began to demand a greater say in the affairs of the country. MPs argued that they represented the important and wealthy members of society and that the monarch should listen to what they had to say.

The dispute between monarch and Parliament became so bitter in the seventeenth century that the two sides went to war and Parliament eventually executed Charles I. For a short time England did not have a king, but in 1660 Charles II, son of the executed king, was restored to the throne.

Which religion?

In the Tudor and Stuart period people took their religion very seriously. As far as most people were concerned, everything that happened to you was in some way connected with God. If you led a good life and pleased God then you prospered; if you upset God then you paid the penalty.

But religion was also very important to the monarchs in helping them to run the country. The Church and its officials played a major role not only in telling people about religion, but also in helping them to form their opinions. If the Church said that the war with France was a good idea then many people would accept this. Therefore monarchs were keen to keep control of religion.

Source B

A portrait of Henry VIII painted in his reign.

Source A

An account by George Fox, the founder of the Quakers, of his visit to Lichfield in 1651.

Immediately the word of the Lord came upon me and told me that I must go to Lichfield.
I was commanded by the Lord to untie my shoes and take them off. The Lord gave me instructions to wander up and down the streets crying in a loud voice 'Woe to the city of Lichfield'. It seemed to me like a channel of blood was running down the streets and the market place was a pool of blood. At first I did not understand this, but later I learned that in Roman times one thousand Christians had been martyred in Lichfield. Then I understood that the Lord had instructed me to walk in my stockings to raise up a memorial of the blood that had been shed over a thousand years earlier.

A portrait of James II painted during his reign.

Everyday life

Whilst all this was going on the vast majority of people went about their daily business untouched by the problems of how the country was to be run or who controlled religion. Most people were involved in farming and worked long hours to achieve a basic standard of living. Of course there were also those who were very rich. These people might have inherited their money or made fortunes in trade. During this period Europeans began to discover previously unknown parts of the world and merchants were quick to trade with the newly discovered lands. The wealth that these merchants accumulated can be seen in the magnificent houses they built for themselves in such places as Hengrave in Suffolk.

So, as you can see, there was plenty going on in this period – and that's without mentioning two of the most famous events of British history which occurred in 1665 and 1666. Do you know what they were?

Power in religion

At the beginning of the Tudor period England was a Catholic country and the Pope was accepted as head of the Church. During the sixteenth century the authority of the Pope was rejected by Parliament and England adopted the new Protestant religion. At the beginning of the seventeenth century groups with extreme beliefs tried to spread their views and had to be kept in check by harsh measures. (Stand by to learn about Quakers, Shakers and Ranters!) By the end of the century the monarchs of England had been forced to accept that they would not follow the Catholic religion and that there were other restrictions on their authority – even though in 1707 England and Wales had officially joined with Scotland to form the United Kingdom.

George Fox

George Fox (1642–91) claimed that God spoke to him when he was nineteen years old and working as an apprentice shoe-maker in Nottingham. He said God told him to tour the country telling the people that they should be guided by their own 'inner light'. He believed that the Church of England had got things wrong.

Not surprisingly these views got Fox into trouble with the authorities and in 1650 he was jailed for blasphemy (speaking disrespectfully about God). At his trial Fox told the judge that he should 'tremble at the word of the Lord'. The judge laughed and called Fox and his followers 'Quakers'. This name has stuck with the group Fox formed, although its correct name is 'The Society of Jesus'.

In Britain today we have many different religions, such as Christianity, Islam and Judaism. People are free to choose which god they want to worship – or whether they want to worship any god at all. So for some people religion plays a major part in their lives and for others it plays almost no part at all. In Tudor times things were very different.

The Church in 1500

In England in 1500 there was only one religion, Christianity, and only one religious organisation, the Catholic Church. The local church was the centre of every village's life and was attended every Sunday and holy day by all the villagers. As it was usually the largest building in the village, it was also where social occasions such as feasts and dances were held – or where some basic schooling was given, though few people could read or write at this time.

Church attendance was very important because people believed that God controlled everything that happened in the world and it was everyone's duty to worship Him. People did not understand why such things as crop failures, disease or drought happened and presumed it was because God was punishing them. So it was important to show proper respect to the Lord. For most people life was short, and around the walls of many churches were pictures reminding them of the pain that awaited them in Hell if they did not lead a good life.

Criticisms of the Church

Although everyone believed strongly in God, this did not stop them from criticising the Church and how it was run. This criticism is called **anti-clericalism** and was often well deserved. Many of the Church officials (such as priests and bishops) were deeply religious and hard-working but there were others who were much less worthy.

Some of the local parish priests could hardly read or write, so they could not conduct the services properly. Others had unofficial 'wives', even though priests were not allowed to marry. Many bishops and abbots lived a life of luxury whilst preaching the need for poverty and self-discipline.

Source A

A report on a monastery in Cambridgeshire by inspectors sent by the King's minister, Thomas Cromwell, in 1535.

Many of the monks devote themselves more to hunting and shooting arrows. Often they wear unsuitable clothes. The abbot is often drunk and some of the monks, especially the older ones, spend much of their time playing gambling games with dice.

A scene from Hell. In this stained glass window from Hengrave Hall in Suffolk, Hell is shown as the mouth of a monster.

Source B

Some of them were bishops or abbots in more than one place and so could not do their jobs properly. In some of the monasteries drinking and gambling were common and the monks paid little attention to their religious duties.

The Pope

The leader of the Church, the Pope, was also open to criticism. There are many examples of popes having children or selling jobs in the Church to people with no religious background. Some people complained that the Pope was a wealthy foreigner who lived in Rome and told English people what to do.

The criticisms of the Church were not limited to England. During the sixteenth century people like Luther in Germany and Calvin in the town of Geneva, in Switzerland, called for changes. They said that the Church should be reformed. Many countries did experience a **Reformation** in their religion at that time and became Protestant. England was one of them, but when change came it began more because of King Henry VIII's personal problems than because of the weaknesses of the Church.

Martin Luther

Martin Luther (1483–1546) was born in Eisleben in Germany, the son of a copper miner. He attended Erfurt University and originally intended to train as a lawyer. However, in 1505 he decided to abandon the study of law and went into an Augustinian monastery. He became a priest in 1507 and began to study theology. By 1510 he had returned to Erfurt University to teach the subject.

In 1510 Luther visited Rome and was appalled by the corruption that he saw there. It was the problems within the Church that led Luther to write his *Ninety-Five Theses* criticizing the way that the Church was run. Luther was summoned to Rome by the pope but refused to go. Eventually he was excommunicated (expelled) from the Church, but continued to write pamphlets criticizing the way religion was run.

Luther's criticisms of the Church are often said to have started the Reformation, when some areas of Europe rejected the Catholic form of religion and set up their own Protestant Church.

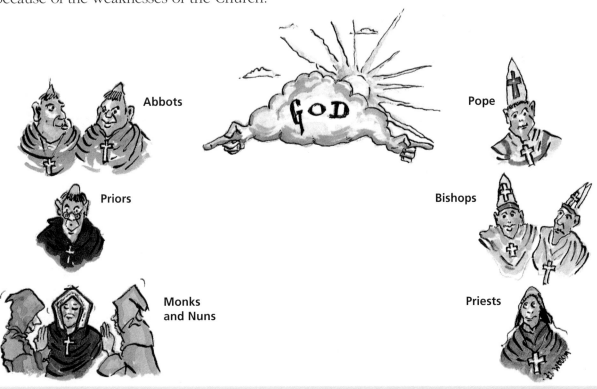

Abbots

Priors

Monks and Nuns

God

Pope

Bishops

Priests

On the left you can see how the monasteries were organised in Tudor times, and on the right how the Catholic Church was organised in Tudor times.

1.3 HENRY VIII AND THE BREAK WITH THE POPE

In 1509 Henry VIII succeeded his father as King of England. He was to rule for 38 years and bring great changes to his country. By his death in 1547 he had been married six times and had also replaced the Pope as head of the Church in England.

Yet in the early years of his reign there was no hint of the dramatic events to follow. Henry was happily married to the Spanish princess, Catherine of Aragon, and was a strong supporter of the Catholic Church. Henry also would not allow criticism of the Church. In Germany, Martin Luther, a teacher at the University of Wittenburg, wrote a series of pamphlets criticising the Catholic Church. Henry had copies of Luther's book publicly burned and wrote his own book criticising Luther's views. Pope Leo X was so impressed that he granted Henry the title 'Defender of the Faith'.

Source A

A portrait of Anne Boleyn painted during her lifetime.

Source B

What Henry gained from the closure of Halesowen Monastery in Worcestershire.

15,000 hectares of arable land

14,000 hectares of pasture

6,500 hectares of meadow

800 hectares of fishing lakes and rivers

800 hectares of woodland

2,000 cottages

6,000 gardens

8 dovecotes [dove houses]

8 windmills

7 watermills

A son and heir

But Henry had problems which were to destroy his marriage and his relationship with the Pope. The King wanted a male heir to succeed him on his death. At this time it was generally agreed that a king should have a son to take over from him when he died. If the king had no son, then a daughter would rule. It was believed that women were not strong enough to control the powerful nobles in the country and stop civil war from breaking out.

However, by 1527 Henry's long-standing marriage with Catherine had produced only one surviving child, a daughter called Mary. Catherine was too old to have any more children and so Henry felt that he had to divorce her and marry a younger woman who could produce the son he needed.

The divorce

In 1527 Henry asked Pope Clement VII for an **annulment** to declare that he had never been properly married to Catherine. It was not particularly unusual for the rulers of Europe to ask for the Pope to annul their marriages and Henry probably expected Clement to grant his request. Unfortunately for him, in the same year that he made his request the Emperor Charles V captured Rome and made the Pope a virtual prisoner. Charles was Catherine's nephew, so he made sure that Clement did not grant the divorce. He did not want to see his aunt treated so badly by Henry.

Struck by the dart of love

Henry was now in a difficult position. For some time he had been pursuing Anne Boleyn, the daughter of a nobleman. In one of his letters to her he said that he was *struck by the dart of love*. He wanted to end his marriage to Catherine and marry Anne. When Anne became pregnant in 1533, Henry became desperate. If he did not marry Anne before she gave birth, their child would be illegitimate and would not be able to succeed to the throne.

Henry insisted that Clement grant the divorce, but the Pope still refused. Therefore Henry instructed the leading Churchman in England, Thomas Cranmer, who was made Archbishop of Canterbury in 1533, to grant the annulment of the marriage himself. When this was done Henry married Anne, crowned her as Queen and awaited the birth of the child which his **astrologers** assured him would be a boy. In September 1533 his hopes were dashed when Anne gave birth to a daughter, Elizabeth.

Henry's six wives, his reasons for marrying them, and how the marriages ended.

Source C

A description of Anne Boleyn by the Venetian Ambassador at Henry's court.

Anne is not one of the handsomest women in the world. She has a swarthy complexion, long neck, wide mouth, bosom not much raised and in fact has little to recommend her except the King's affection and her eyes, which are black and beautiful. She has very long black hair which she wears loose.

Catherine of Aragon

Catherine (1485–1536) was Henry VIII's first wife and mother of Mary I. She first married Henry's brother, Arthur in 1501, but when he died she married Henry.

She gave birth to six children, but only one survived. The failure to have a son was a major factor in Henry's decision to divorce Catherine in 1533. After the divorce she retired from public life.

A son is born

Henry's marriage to Anne lasted just three years before he had her beheaded in 1536. At one point Henry accused her of having had over 1000 lovers and of practising witchcraft. But her real 'crime' was failing to produce a baby boy. Henry's next wife, Jane Seymour, did produce a son, Edward, in 1537, but she died giving birth. Henry was to have three more wives, but no more children.

Henry had divorced Catherine without the agreement of the Pope. He now decided that the time had come to make a formal break with Rome. He was a determined ruler who did not like opposition to his rule and had come to resent the authority a foreign Pope had in England.

Henry as Supreme Head

Henry summoned Parliament in 1529 and encouraged it to attack the Pope and the Church. In 1534 he had Parliament declare him Supreme Head of the Church of England. This meant that the Pope no longer had any say in how religion was to be run in England. Henry was in charge, but in 1535 he handed over the management of religion and the Church to his leading minister, Thomas Cromwell (1480–1540). Henry demanded that everyone support his new title, and executed such people as Thomas More, a leading Catholic, for opposing him.

Monasteries and nunneries

Next Henry turned his attention to the religious houses in England. For centuries the monasteries and nunneries had played an important part not only in Catholic religious life, but also in the care of the sick and the poor and in education. But they were now facing heavy criticism. Monks and nuns were accused of neglecting their religious obligations and of greed and laziness. There was also widespread resentment of the wealth of religious houses. Some monasteries owned huge areas of land, which they rented out at great profit, or had valuable gold and silver treasures.

Source D

A contemporary woodcut showing Henry VIII trampling on the Pope.

Jane Seymour

Born in 1508, the daughter of John and Marjory Seymour, Jane Seymour became the third wife of King Henry VIII. They were married on 20 May 1536 in Wiltshire when Jane was 28 and Henry was 45. The King had first shown an interest in Jane in 1534. She was certainly the type of woman he preferred – short, with a small, childlike face. Jane gave birth to Henry's only son, the future Edward VI, on 12 October 1537.

The King was thrilled. However, Jane tragically died only twelve days after the birth. Out of respect for her as the mother of his son, Henry arranged to have himself buried next to Jane when he died.

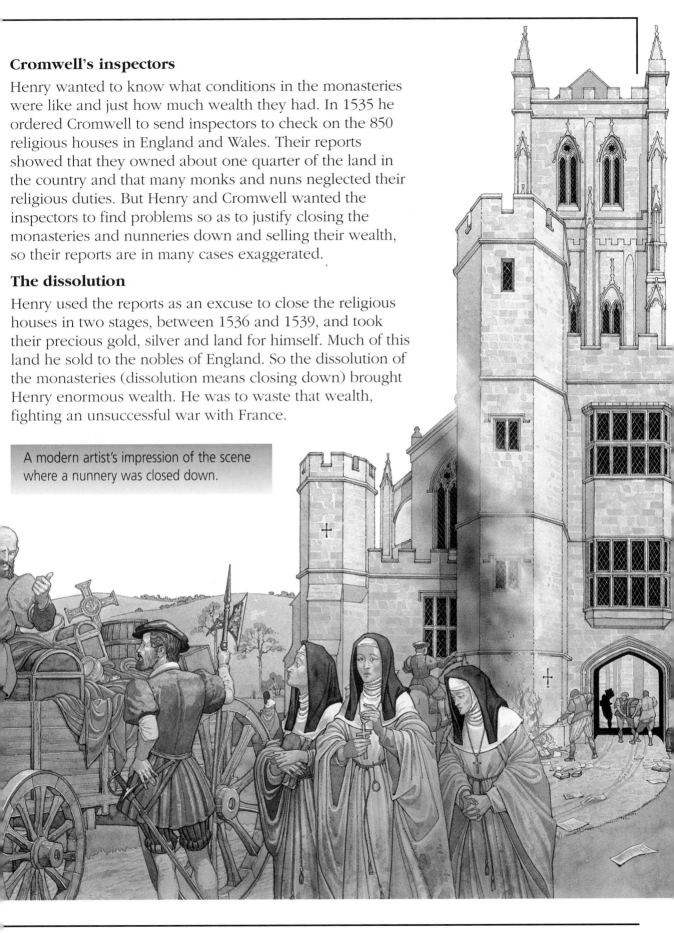

Cromwell's inspectors

Henry wanted to know what conditions in the monasteries were like and just how much wealth they had. In 1535 he ordered Cromwell to send inspectors to check on the 850 religious houses in England and Wales. Their reports showed that they owned about one quarter of the land in the country and that many monks and nuns neglected their religious duties. But Henry and Cromwell wanted the inspectors to find problems so as to justify closing the monasteries and nunneries down and selling their wealth, so their reports are in many cases exaggerated.

The dissolution

Henry used the reports as an excuse to close the religious houses in two stages, between 1536 and 1539, and took their precious gold, silver and land for himself. Much of this land he sold to the nobles of England. So the dissolution of the monasteries (dissolution means closing down) brought Henry enormous wealth. He was to waste that wealth, fighting an unsuccessful war with France.

A modern artist's impression of the scene where a nunnery was closed down.

Fountains Abbey is a famous Cistercian Abbey in North Yorkshire. By the time of the dissolution of the monasteries it had become one of the richest abbeys in the whole of England. The dates given below show how long it lasted. But did it deserve to close?

Source A

Fountains Abbey, North Yorkshire.

The rise and fall of Fountains Abbey

1132	Abbey founded with thirteen monks.
1133	Abbey becomes part of Cistercian order.
1150–1200	Gifts of land from local landowners make the abbey rich. Abbey has enormous sheep flocks and lead and iron deposits. Extensive rebuilding takes place.
1200–65	Fountains becomes the richest Cistercian Abbey in England.
1300–99	Monks begin to eat meat when not ill. Estates are run by hired servants or rented out.
1495–1526	Number of monks rises to fifty-two.
1536	Abbot Thirsk forced to resign by Cromwell's inspectors. Marmaduke Bradley pays to become abbot.
1539	Abbot Bradley and monks surrender abbey to King. Treasure taken to royal treasury, but buildings left intact.
1540	Abbey stripped of lead, timber and glass. Abbey sold to a London merchant, Sir Richard Gresham (1517–79).

Cistercian beliefs

The Cistercians were amongst the strictest orders of monks. They followed the beliefs of the monastic founder St Benedict (480–547) which said:

1 Monks should follow vows of poverty, chastity and obedience.

2 Monks' days should be divided into the working part, the studying part and the praying part.

3 Monasteries should serve God through worship, charity work, hospitality to travellers and providing education.

But Cistercians had even stricter views. Their founder, Robert, Abbot of Cîteaux, said that they should have extra rules. Here are some of them:

1 Isolation: monasteries should be well away from civilisation.

2 Self-sufficiency: monks should not accept outside help or rent out land. Instead they should live by the fruits of their own labour on the land.

3 Vegetarianism: monks should not eat meat unless they were ill.

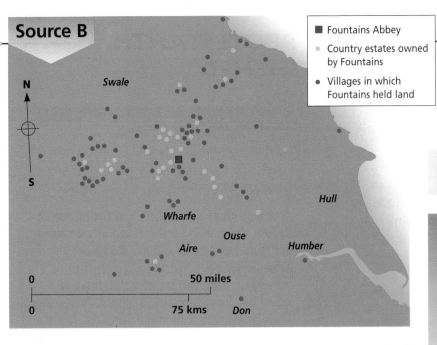

■ Fountains Abbey
● Country estates owned by Fountains
● Villages in which Fountains held land

Swale

N

S

0   50 miles

0   75 kms

Wharfe

Aire   Ouse

Hull

Humber

Don

A map of land in Yorkshire owned by Fountains Abbey.

Source D

In 1536 a Catholic lawyer, Robert Aske, led a huge demonstration in the north of England against the dissolution of the monasteries. This is part of his speech explaining why he disapproved of the King's actions.

The abbeys in the North gave charity to poor men and served God in a commendable way. Now these temples of God are pulled down and there is no hospitality in these parts. These abbeys were things of beauty and places where young men could give service to God or young daughters be brought up in virtue.

Source C

Extracts from inspectors' reports sent to Thomas Cromwell in 1536.

The Abbot of Fountains has greatly ruined his abbey, wasting his woodland and keeping six mistresses. Six days before our arrival he committed theft. At midnight he went with a local goldsmith and removed a great emerald and ruby from a gold cross. The goldsmith bought the emerald and ruby and some silver. The abbot is truly a fool and a miserable idiot and has resigned.

There is a monk at the abbey called Marmaduke. He is the wisest monk within England and well educated. He is a wealthy fellow who will pay 600 marks (£400) to be made abbot. We think this man suitable for the post.

Robert Aske

Robert Aske was the leader of an uprising against Henry VIII, called the Pilgrimage of Grace. We know very little about his early life, except that he was probably born near Richmond, in Yorkshire, and then trained as a lawyer in London.

The Pilgrimage of Grace began in Lincolnshire in October 1536 when 10,000 protesters marched on Lincoln and beat to death some Church officials. The protesters were angry at the way that Henry VIII was closing monasteries. However, when Henry send an army led by the Duke of Suffolk, the rebels quickly melted away. But at the same time thousands of 'pilgrims' began a march asking the King to stop closing the monasteries.

The King's representative, the Duke of Norfolk, agreed to discuss the pilgrims' complaints with the King. The pilgrims returned home, thinking that they had won a victory.

Yet Henry was just waiting for an opportunity to strike. This came in January 1537 when new revolts broke out in Yorkshire, led by Robert Aske. Royal forces quickly put down the rebellion and 74 rebels were hanged as a warning to others. Then the leaders were arrested and tried for treason. Amongst those executed was Robert Aske, even though it was believed that he had tried to stop the protesters from rebelling against Henry.

Henry VIII and Cromwell began the process by which England became a Protestant country. In 1547 Henry died. The new King, Henry's son Edward VI, was only nine years old. He had been brought up as a Protestant but England was not yet a fully Protestant country. The main church service was still the Catholic Mass, said in Latin, the language of the Catholic Church.

Because Edward was so young the country was run by senior nobles, firstly the Duke of Somerset and later the Duke of Northumberland. Both of them were strong Protestants. So it was during Edward's short reign that England finally became a Protestant country (see the box below).

Edward falls ill

Not everyone agreed with the religious changes. The new prayer book was very unpopular. Three bishops were dismissed for refusing to use it and there was a serious rebellion against it in Cornwall in 1549. Yet the main threat to the Protestant religion was not rebels, but the King's poor health. In 1553 Edward was dying from **tuberculosis**. The heir to the throne was Mary, who was a devout Catholic and daughter of the discarded Catherine of Aragon. To save Protestantism the Duke of Northumberland decided he would try to stop Mary becoming Queen.

Source A

An account of Lady Jane Grey's execution, from the *Chronicle of Two Years of Queen Mary*, written during the reign of Mary Tudor.

Kneeling down she recited a psalm in a most devout manner. Then she stood up and gave her maid her gloves and handkerchief. The executioner gave her a handkerchief to tie around her eyes before he knelt down and asked her forgiveness. She gave it most willingly. Then he asked her to stand upon the straw and in doing so she saw the block. She said 'Please despatch me quickly'. Then feeling for the block she cried 'What shall I do? Where is it?' A bystander guided her to the block and she lay her head upon it and said 'Lord, into thy hands I commend my spirit'. And so she ended.

Guildford Dudley

Guildford Dudley (1534–54) was married to Lady Jane Grey in May 1553. The wedding was planned so hastily that Jane had to borrow a dress from the Royal Wardrobe. Guildford was the son of John Dudley, the Duke of Northumberland. Northumberland clearly hoped that if his plan to make Jane Queen succeeded, then his son would become King.

This plan was to have tragic consequences, as it resulted in Guildford being executed, along with his young wife. Guildford was beheaded at the Tower of London on 12 February 1554, aged 20.

Steps by which England became Protestant under Edward VI

1547 Archbishop Thomas Cranmer issued a book of Protestant sermons which had to be read in all churches. All chantries (chapels where prayers can be said for the dead) were dissolved and much of the income used to found schools. (Many King Edward VI schools still exist today.)

1548 The government ordered that images such as statues and paintings in churches should be removed.

1549 A new prayer book, written in English by Archbishop Cranmer, was issued. This set out the service which all churches had to follow and included the instruction that priests should wear plain clothes.

No music, statues or stained glass windows. No brightly coloured clothing, dancing, theatres or drinking to excess.

We want: long sermons based on the Bible, a God-fearing life, more schools and colleges, help for the poor.

Puritan beliefs.

Catholic plots

During the 1580s, as relations between England and Catholic Spain grew worse, measures against Catholics became even harsher, particularly when plots to overthrow Elizabeth and replace her with her Catholic cousin, Mary Queen of Scots, were discovered. Between 1577 and 1603, 183 Catholics were executed – including Mary in 1587.

The Puritans

The Catholics did not like Elizabeth's religious policy because it was too Protestant. There was another group, however, the Puritans, who wanted the Church to be even more Protestant. This group was extremely influential and had supporters amongst government officials such as Sir Walter Mildmay, the Chancellor of the Exchequer. Elizabeth once described the Puritans as greater enemies than the Catholics. Elizabeth took measures against the Puritans but was not able to wipe out this group – which proved even more troublesome for the Stuart kings of the next century.

Mary, Queen of Scots

Mary Stuart was born in 1542, the only daughter of James V, King of Scotland, and his French wife, Mary of Guise. James died just a week after Mary's death, and Mary was sent to be brought up in France. There she married the Dauphin (heir to the throne) in 1558. He became King Francis II in 1559, but on his death in 1560 Mary returned to Scotland. She was a Catholic, but in her absence Scotland had become a Protestant country, so there was a great deal of opposition to her.

In 1565 Mary married Lord Darnley, but he died two years later in a mysterious explosion. Mary then caused uproar by marrying the Earl of Bothwell, who was thought to have organized Darnley's death! The Scottish nobles rose up against Mary and forced her to abdicate. She fled to England where Elizabeth decided to keep her a prisoner. It was too risky to allow a Catholic rival to remain free. But in 1586 she was found guilty of plotting against Elizabeth and was executed in 1587.

Source B

A priesthole in the 'King's Room', Moseley Old Hall, Staffordshire.

MARGARET CLITHEROW

Margaret Clitherow was a butcher's wife from York who was executed for her religious beliefs in March 1586. She was a recusant who had sheltered Catholic priests in her house. One of her servants betrayed her and she was arrested. She refused to stand trial because she thought that her children would be forced to give evidence against her. The punishment for refusing to stand trial was death by crushing. On the day of her execution the local officials hired four beggars to carry out her execution, even though they were supposed to do it themselves. She was tied down, face upwards, and a large sharp stone put underneath her. Then a door was placed over her and heavy stones placed on top. Eventually her body was crushed and she died.

The building of the Hall

In 1520 a rich cloth merchant called Thomas Kytson purchased the manor of Hengrave in Suffolk. Four years later he began replacing the old building with the fine hall which stands at Hengrave today. By 1538 the Hall was finished along with its vineyard, fish ponds and gardens completed in the latest fashionable Dutch style. Kytson's successful trading had allowed his family to 'make it' in Elizabethan society.

But Kytson had little time to enjoy his newly built home, as he died in 1540. The Hall passed to his widow, Margaret Donnington, who in the same year gave birth to a son, also called Thomas Kytson. Margaret married twice more and her third husband was a strong supporter of Mary Tudor. When Mary fled from London to avoid capture by Northumberland in 1553 (see page 15) she spent some of her time at Hengrave Hall.

Jane Paget, the first wife of Thomas Kytson, the younger, died after just one year of marriage. In 1560 Thomas married Elizabeth Cornwallis. When Thomas' mother died in 1561 Thomas and Elizabeth settled in Hengrave Hall.

The wrong religion

The history of the Kytson family provides us with a fascinating insight into how Catholics were treated at this time. Elizabeth Kytson's godmother was the Duchess of Norfolk. The Norfolk family was the most important Catholic family in England, and Elizabeth remained a staunch Catholic throughout her life. Thomas Kytson was also a Catholic and spent time in prison. But Sources C and D show he tried hard not to fall out with the authorities and was prepared to agree to follow Protestant practices to make sure he remained in the Queen's good books.

Source A

Hengrave Hall as it is today.

Back in favour

Kytson's efforts were obviously successful as in August 1578 Queen Elizabeth came to stay at Hengrave Hall. We are told by Thomas Churchyard, who witnessed the scene that:

There were 200 young gentlemen, clad in white velvet and 300 in black velvet and 1500 more on horseback ready to receive the Queen. The banquet did so exceed that at other places. A show representing the fairies was seen and a rich jewel was presented to the Queen.

Queen Elizabeth must have been suitably impressed because during her visit she knighted Thomas Kytson.

In trouble again

The Kytsons ran into trouble again in Queen Elizabeth's reign and by 1588 they were both on a list of local recusants. Elizabeth Kytson had to spend time in prison for refusing to attend Protestant services.

It is interesting to see that even though the Kytsons appeared to be constantly under suspicion, they do not seem to have suffered any long-lasting harm as a result of having 'the wrong religion'. Their property was not confiscated and their lives were not threatened. Thomas died a very wealthy man in 1602 and his wife continued to live at Hengrave until her death in 1628 at the age of 81 – a grand old age for those times.

Perhaps it was because the Kytsons were so wealthy that they escaped some of the harsh penalties which lower-class Catholics suffered in the later years of Elizabeth's reign. In Tudor times, wealth and good connections often enabled people to get away with things that poorer people could not.

Source B

The Kytson coat of arms.

Source C

Thomas Kytson writing to the Duke of Norfolk after hearing of a complaint made against him to the authorities.

I understand that I am accused of saying that the present religion is based on what my Lord Keeper and Secretary Cecil want, not what her Majesty the Queen wants and that she is indifferent in matters of religion. I have good cause to deny the whole of this matter as a thing I never even thought, and therefore certainly never said.

I told the Lord Keeper that I was most unfairly **slandered** and begged him to suspend his judgement of me. He said he would think about the matter before deciding. I told him that he was welcome to stay at my house on his travels. He said that if he found the complaint against me to be untrue he would come to my house, otherwise he would not.

Source D

A letter written at the beginning of Elizabeth's reign by Thomas Kytson apologising to the Queen for his previous behaviour and promising to behave himself in future! In fact, he failed to keep his promise to attend Protestant services.

I have been in prison since last September. Now being asked about my views on religion I say that the answer I gave then was because I did not know as much about the situation as I do now.

I do protest and promise to your Highness that I am thoroughly persuaded to obey the laws on religion, according to my duty, without any **conceit** (which I have previously shown). Neither will I be lazy or negligent, as I have been, in listening to sermons, reading books and hearing the arguments of wise and learned men.

Behind the scenes of the Hall

The Kytsons are very useful for telling us about the sort of life led by important families at this time.

We know that the Kytsons were very important people both in their local community and nationally. They were **patrons** of music and maintained a permanent band of musicians at Hengrave Hall. Both Thomas Kytson and his wife were accomplished lute players and their daughters were also skilled musicians. The family's account books are full of references to payments made to musicians (see Source E), and an inventory of the house lists numerous chests full of musical instruments.

An indication of the wealth of the family can be seen in the portrait of Lady Kytson. She is wearing the latest highly expensive fashion. Bright colours had become fashionable at this time and her sleeves are embroidered with roses, honeysuckle and carnations. Her gown is trimmed with fur and her hat has a jewelled band.

Elizabeth Kytson was a woman of strong character who was well thought of by those who came into contact with her. She spent some time in the household of her godmother, the Duchess of Norfolk, an important Catholic, aristocratic woman. When she left the house of the Duchess of Norfolk to marry Thomas, the Duchess wrote to her mother saying: *I must desire you, good Madam, to let me have Bess [Elizabeth] again. I would gladly keep her with me until her marriage.*

Elizabeth's father also wrote to her on one occasion asking her to sort out a quarrel between her brothers.

Source F

Elizabeth Cornwallis, Lady Kytson, painted by the Elizabethan artist George Gower in 1573 when Lady Kytson was 26 years old.

The tomb of Thomas Kytson, Elizabeth Kytson and Jane Paget.

The inscription states that Sir Thomas
Departed this life the 28 January 1602 and in the year of his age 63. This monument was erected at ye charge of Dame Elizabeth Kytson, in memory of her beloved husband, 20 September 1608.

Note how Thomas' first wife, Jane, is pushed into the corner!

Source H

Some of the charitable donations made by Elizabeth Kytson.

In 1625 Elizabeth endowed the almshouses at Hengrave with £30 or so a year that the poor could live there.

In 1626 she endowed the manor of Lackford with £4 a year to give 12 poor people clothes on All Saints Day every year.

In her will in 1628 Elizabeth left all her servants 40 shillings.

The Duke and Duchess of Norfolk

The Duke and Duchess of Norfolk were close friends of the Kytsons, both couples being well-to-do recusants in East Anglia. Elizabeth spent many years working in the household of the Duchess, as this was the normal way for young gentry girls to 'learn the trade' of being a gentry woman. When Elizabeth and Thomas announced they were to be married, the Duke of Norfolk insisted that their marriage should take place at Kenninghall, the Norfolks' house.

However, this friendship also got the Kytsons into trouble. The Norfolks were well-known Catholics, and when the Duke was finally punished for his recusancy, Thomas pleaded with the Queen not to let the Duke's situation 'hinder your Majesty's good opinion of me'.

Her father obviously saw her as strong woman because he suggested that Elizabeth should *Imagine for the time they be your children. Use the authority I have given you, good Bess and remember, soft surgery makes foul sores.*

Elizabeth was also a kind woman who did not neglect her duty to help the poor, as Source H shows.

The records from Hengrave Hall make it possible for us to see a wealthy Tudor family's life as it really was. Thomas and Elizabeth Kytson were important people in Elizabethan England and the government tried hard to ensure that they 'toed the line' when it came to religion. For long periods the Kytsons must have been concerned that their Catholicism might lead to their downfall.

At the same time they seem to have lived life to the full and to have continued with the important task of raising their daughters, Margaret and Mary, in a style which reflected the fact that the Kytsons were a family who had 'made it' in Tudor England.

2.1 PARLIAMENT – MORE POWER TO THE PEOPLE?

Parliament today

Parliament today has a very important role in running the country. The Queen is officially the Head of State, but in reality the country is run by 'Her Majesty's Government'. That government is chosen from the political party which has the most MPs, as members of the House of Commons are called. Government business and proposed laws are debated in the House of Commons and the House of Lords (which together are called Parliament) before they can become law.

There are strict rules about how our Parliament works. It is divided into two separate groups. The House of Lords is made up of people who have either been born into a title (such as Duke) or been given a title by the Queen. The members of the House of Commons are elected by the people of the country. Almost everyone aged eighteen years or over can vote and there must be a General Election at least every five years. The leader of the winning party becomes the Prime Minister and appoints other Ministers to important government jobs.

Tudor parliaments

In Tudor times Parliament did not meet regularly. Instead it was only called when the monarch wanted to pass laws or get permission for taxes to be collected. Parliament did not run the country. That job was done by the monarch and the council of 20–30 senior government members chosen by the king or queen.

There was a House of Lords with its members chosen in the same way as today, but the House of Commons was very different. Today there are nearly 700 MPs. In 1485 there were fewer than 300. These members saw their job not as representing the people of their area, but as ensuring that the rights of the wealthy were protected. Elections were rare, since if two people wanted to be the MP for the same place, one of them usually stood down. If an election was held, only the wealthy were permitted to vote. Ordinary people had no say in who became an MP, and women were not allowed to vote or stand as MPs.

Source A

A scene from Parliament in the 1990s.

Changing Parliament

Henry VII called his parliaments very rarely. Since he did not introduce many new laws and tried to avoid foreign wars, he had no need to call Parliament to make laws or raise taxation.

In the reign of Henry VIII, however, there was a significant change in the importance of Parliament. The changes that Henry was making in religion were so serious that he wanted the backing of Parliament for what he was doing. The 'break from Rome' was to be achieved by a series of laws passed in Parliament. So during Henry's reign of 56 years there were almost as many laws passed as there had been in the previous 300 years. His Reformation Parliament of 1529–36 met for 78 weeks – more than Parliament had met in the whole of Henry VII's reign! Under Henry VIII Parliament became much more a 'partner' in government than it had been before.

Yet at the same time Parliament also became much more willing to criticise the monarch's actions and to stand up for its own rights. In 1523 Henry VIII's Chief Minister, Wolsey, asked the Speaker of the House of Commons to stop MPs from complaining about how the King was acting. The Speaker replied: *I have neither eyes to see nor ears to hear except as the House directs me, I am its servant.* Since all opposition was reported straight back to Henry and an angry Henry VIII was a frightening sight, it must have taken great courage to stand up to the King in Parliament!

Source B

Henry VIII sitting at the head of Parliament.

Thomas Wolsey

Wolsey (1475–1530) was one of Henry VIII's most trusted advisors. Although he came from a poor background he held many important offices. By 1515 he had been appointed a Cardinal by the Pope and Lord Chancellor by Henry. He also built the magnificent palace at Hampton Court.

But when he failed to get Henry his divorce from Catherine of Aragon his enemies had him charged with treason. He died in 1530 on his way to London to stand trial.

Relations with Parliament

In the reigns of Edward and Mary, Parliament continued to be important. During Edward's reign some important laws were passed to control food prices. Soon merchants realised that it would be in their best interests to join together to make proposals to Parliament. This **lobbying** is very common today and groups such as Greenpeace and trade unions often meet MPs to explain their views to them.

Historians disagree about the importance of Parliament in the reign of Elizabeth. Some of them believe that a small group of very influential MPs carried out a constant attack on Elizabeth's policies. Others think that there was no real disagreement between Elizabeth and her parliaments, and that generally there was great co-operation between them. There were times when Elizabeth thought that Parliament went too far and she criticised troublesome MPs. But since she was in constant need of money from Parliament, she could not treat it in the same way as her father had. By the end of the sixteenth century, Parliament had become very important in helping run the country, and Elizabeth's ministers worked hard to make sure that relations between the Queen's government and Parliament were usually very good.

Sir William Petre

Sir William Petre is a good example of how a loyal and hard-working Member of Parliament could make an excellent career in government.

He was born in 1506 and at the age of fourteen went to Oxford University, to study law. He became friendly with Anne Boleyn's father, George, who helped him gain a job at Court, and he was one of the lawyers working on Henry VIII's divorce from Catherine of Aragon. In 1536 Petre was appointed as deputy to Thomas Cromwell, whose job it was to inspect the monasteries of England. In the same year he was elected to Parliament, and he was an MP through the reigns of Henry VIII, Edward, Mary and Elizabeth.

In 1544 Petre was appointed Principal Secretary to Henry VIII and he continued to hold that office for the next thirteen years. During Edward's reign he was responsible for checking that no 'unacceptable books' were published. A law of 1549 stated that *No printer shall print any English book unless it has been examined by Mr Petre, Mr Smith or Mr Cecil.* Another of Petre's tasks was to try to persuade Princess Mary to give up her Catholicism. She refused.

Source C

A comment on relations between Parliament and Elizabeth, written by a modern historian.

Elizabeth adopted a tone of superiority towards her parliaments, confident that if she explained things often enough and slowly enough the little boys would understand. For Elizabeth MPs were little boys – sometimes unruly, usually a nuisance and always a waste of an intelligent woman's time. Queen Elizabeth did not like parliaments – and it showed.

Source D

Part of a speech by the MP Peter Wentworth in 1576. Elizabeth was angry when it was reported to her. She said it was monstrous that the feet should direct the head. Wentworth was imprisoned for a month.

Among other things, Mr Speaker, two things do greatly hurt in this place of which I mean to speak. One is the rumour which runs about the House that Her Majesty does not like certain things and whoever speaks of them she will be angry with. The other is that Her Majesty does like certain matters and whoever speaks against them will greatly offend her. This goes against the practice of free speech. It is a dangerous thing in a Queen to treat and abuse people as Her Majesty did in the last parliament.

Despite their disagreements Mary re-appointed Petre as one of her Principal Secretaries when she became Queen in 1553. He finally resigned this post in 1557 because of ill health. But he did continue to carry out tasks for the government in the reigns of both Mary and Elizabeth, who asked him to take charge of Lady Catherine Grey, the sister of Jane and a possible rival to Elizabeth for the throne of England.

Sir William was not a healthy man and his account books show that payments were made regularly to leading apothecaries and physicians (see page 32). He is known to have suffered a variety of medical problems including **varicose veins**, an ulcerated leg, kidney stones and a rupture, but he did manage to avoid smallpox, which was a very common disease in Tudor London. It seems that throughout his time in Parliament and working for the various monarchs, he was constantly struggling against ill health. In 1565 he wrote to a friend in government:

I have recovered from fever, but am still a little deaf. I am really unfit for public office. As soon as I am well enough I shall go by litter to my country home with such remedies as the physicians do prepare for me for the pain I have from my head to my shoulders. I am persuaded that the open air will do me good.

William's health was failing, but he lived a further seven years until his death on 13 January 1572. His widow, Lady Anne Petre, was his second wife and was an interesting character in her own right. She was a devout Catholic and after William's death had several priestholes built in the family home, Ingatestone Hall. There she hid the priest John Payne, but he was arrested in 1577 and exiled. He returned to the Hall but was betrayed by a servant, re-arrested and executed in 1582. Lady Anne died just one week later.

Source E

Sir William Petre.

Ingatestone Hall

Ingatestone Hall was the home of Sir William Petre and his family. He built the fine Tudor manor house in 1540, whilst he was working for Thomas Cromwell. The house has hardly been altered since, except for the enlargement of the windows.

Luckily for historians, the Petres of Ingatestone left behind a great many letters, account books, and everyday documents which provide a fascinating insight into the life of a wealthy family in Tudor England.

Although Elizabeth I was one of England's most popular and successful monarchs, there are very few written accounts of what she looked like from her lifetime.

Of course it ought to be easy to tell exactly what Elizabeth looked like because we have numerous portraits of her painted during her lifetime. Unfortunately things are not that simple. Elizabeth's father, Henry VIII, had ensured that his portraits showed him in the best possible light. Elizabeth adopted the same policy. After all, in a time when there was no television or newspapers and when travel was very difficult, few people would ever see the Queen. If all they knew of Elizabeth's looks was what they saw in paintings, then it was important to make sure that those paintings reflected Elizabeth in a good light.

Source A

A portrait of Elizabeth as a young girl, painted in 1546.

Source B

A portrait of Elizabeth painted in 1583.

Source C

A portrait of Elizabeth painted in 1600.

Source D

A portrait of Elizabeth painted in 1588 to celebrate the defeat of the Spanish Armada.

Source E

A portrait of Elizabeth in her final years. It was, in fact, painted some years after her death.

Source F

Orders issued in 1563 by William Cecil, Elizabeth's Secretary of State.

No painter, printer or engraver shall draw Her Majesty's picture until some especially able painter might be permitted access to Her Majesty to make a natural representation. The painter shall finish a portrait after which Her Majesty will be content that all other painters shall follow the same pattern in their portraits.

Source G

A description of Elizabeth by the Venetian ambassador in 1574.

Her face is comely rather than handsome, but she is tall and well formed, with a good skin, though rather swarthy. She has fine eyes.

Source H

A description of Elizabeth by a foreign visitor in 1598.

Her face is oblong, fair but wrinkled, her eyes small, yet black and pleasant, her nose is a little hooked, her lips narrow, topped with an auburn wig.

Tudor make-up

In order to look her best, Elizabeth used lots of cosmetics, but the make-up known in Tudor times was very different from make-up today! The Elizabethans believed that the perfect woman should have a pale, white face, with bright red lips and cheeks, large, bright eyes, and sparkling white teeth. (This last requirement was very difficult as there were no dentists in Tudor times.)

To make her face white, Elizabeth used a powder of white lead. We now know that this is extremely poisonous, and causes open sores! To make her lips and cheeks cherry red, Elizabeth used cochineal, which is made from crushed beetles. Cochineal is still used today as a food colouring. Drops of belladonna were put in Elizabeth's eyes to make them look bright and shining. Belladonna is from an extremely poisonous plant known as deadly nightshade. As Elizabeth got older she lost her famous red hair, and started wearing a wig.

Tudor women did not bathe often, and so the attractive effect of all their make-up could often be lost by the smell of their unwashed bodies. Strong perfumes from the East were used to disguise this. It is even said that Elizabeth used to put apples under her armpits to try to hide the smell of her sweat!

One of the major differences between Tudor England and England at the end of the twentieth century is that in Tudor times the vast majority of people lived in the countryside. London, with a population of over 100,000, was considered to be a huge city. The next largest towns were Norwich, the centre of the textile industry, Bristol, a major port, and York, the major city in the north of England. Yet none of these had a population of more than 20,000 – what we today think of as just a small town.

Farming the land

In the countryside almost everyone had a job connected with agriculture. Most of the land was owned by the nobility and gentry who would rent it out to tenants, who employed the local peasants to work the land. Life for most peasants was very harsh and they often worked from dawn to dusk for very low wages. They also owned small strips of land in the village, on which they could grow their own food. All villagers also had the right to graze their livestock on the 'common land'.

During the Tudor period more and more land was enclosed, so that crops could be grown or livestock such as sheep could be raised more efficiently. Historians are uncertain about the effects of enclosure on the peasants, but we do know that some villagers were badly hit. This was because sometimes the peasants' land or the common land was enclosed by unscrupulous landowners, or simply because fewer people were needed to look after sheep than to grow crops. Therefore some peasants lost their jobs.

Although life in the countryside was hard work for the ordinary peasants, there were always the holy days (holidays) to look forward to. May Day was a great opportunity for drinking, dancing and engaging in cock-fighting or football.

Source A

A picture showing the type of work done in a Tudor village.

Towns

Tudor towns were very different to the way towns are today. There were no cars, so the streets did not need to be so wide. Sometimes houses were crammed so close together that people could touch each other across the street from their windows. Rubbish was thrown out of the window or into local rivers and ditches. This rubbish included human waste because there were no flushing toilets. Disease was common – a quarter of children born died before the age of ten.

Poor people might share a house with up to fifteen people living in one room! Rich people's houses were less cramped. They might have as many as fifteen rooms in a building with five floors.

Larger towns had market places where people from the countryside came to sell their produce. Farmers might bring sheep or cattle. Their wives might bring milk or eggs. Market day was a busy day and as well as

people selling things there were those who, for a small sum, would pull out bad teeth or cut people's hair. There were also those who would happily pick a pocket or start a fight. Punishments were very severe in Tudor times, but market day was often a day when plenty of ale was drunk and riotous behaviour followed.

Beer, beer and more beer!

Tudor people drank a lot more beer than people do now. It was believed in Tudor times that water drunk alone was bad for you, and with good cause, since the water supplies were often very dirty. So instead of water, the Tudors drank beer, or ale. Children and adults alike would drink ale with every meal. The children would drink 'small ale', a weaker kind of beer, to stop them getting drunk! On the Tudor war ship, the *Mary Rose*, soldiers' rations included eight pints of beer ... a day!

In Tudor times, four types of people provided medical treatment:

1 Wealthy people could call out a licensed **physician**. This was a man who had been educated at university, often for up to fourteen years. Physicians charged high fees, but despite their long period of study their real knowledge of medicine and the human body was very limited compared with what we know today.

2 Physicians thought that surgery was an unskilled job which was beneath them. So this task was carried out by surgeons, who often combined the task with the trade of a barber, so they were called **barber-surgeons**. People saw no reason why those who cut hair should not also carry out amputation of limbs!

3 Next in rank were **apothecaries**, who were like modern-day chemists. They prepared medicines for physicians as well as selling their own direct to patients.

4 A fourth type was the **midwife**, who assisted women during childbirth. Since women were not allowed to attend university they could not become physicians, so this was one of the few areas of medicine open to them.

Most people could not afford to use any of these trained people. Instead they were treated by unlicensed or amateur physicians. In 1542 Henry VIII's Parliament passed an act allowing *diverse honest persons* to practise medicine. These people ranged from those who based their treatment on herbal cures to those who were definitely not 'honest persons' and made a living from tricking people.

A French painting showing a sick person being 'touched' by King Henry II. It was widely believed that some illnesses, such as the skin disease scrofula, could be cured by being touched by the monarch.

Bile and blood-letting

In Tudor times no one was really sure how the body worked and there were no **anaesthetics** to kill pain or **antiseptics** to kill germs (not that anyone had ever heard of them!). So operations were painful and dangerous and often resulted in the death of the patient.

Most physicians still accepted the views of the Greek doctor Galen, who lived in the second century AD, that good health depended upon the correct balance of the four humours: yellow bile, phlegm, black bile and blood. Disease occurred if the humours got out of balance and had to be corrected by treatments such as blood-letting (by opening a vein or using leeches) and purging (by using strong laxatives).

Source A

Medicine and the stars

Another belief which influenced medical practice at this time was astrology. By studying the stars it was thought possible to decide when was the best time to treat a patient. The moon was considered very important in making decisions about surgery or blood-letting.

Regardless of the depth of medical knowledge amongst physicians, most people relied on medical practices that had been passed down for generations. The local village wise woman with her knowledge of herbs was much more likely to treat an illness successfully than any other person.

LADY GRACE MILDMAY

Lady Grace Mildmay was born in 1552 near Chippenham in Wiltshire. She had wealthy but strict parents who were keen to ensure that she had proper religious guidance. She was allowed to read only four books (amongst them the Bible and Foxe's *Book of Martyrs*). In 1567 she married Anthony Mildmay, son of a wealthy merchant. Mildmay was not keen on the marriage and spent much time away from home. In his absence Lady Mildmay spent her time bible reading, playing the lute, caring for the sick and doing embroidery. In 1582 she gave birth to her only child, Mary.

Lady Grace Mildmay was one of a number of women of the upper classes in Elizabethan times who became interested in practising medicine and who drew up a list of recipes of potions for curing illnesses. She seems to have read the works of established medical authorities of the time and she based a lot of her views of medicine on Christian teaching. She was a devout Puritan and believed that human sin caused illness. She devised a number of treatments for many problems, from smallpox and madness to ringworm and even unwanted pregnancies.

Although she had received no proper training, she came to know a great deal about medicine and was probably better at treating illness than most physicians.

Source B

A Tudor cure for tuberculosis, the disease which killed King Edward VI.

Take a sow pig of nine days old and put her in a tank with a handful of spearmint, half a handful of turnip, a handful of celery, nine dates and two crushed sticks of good cinnamon. Put this over a fire and get the juice out of it. Then put the juice in a glass and stand it in the sun for nine days, then drink nine spoonfuls of it at once.

Source C

An extract from the account book for 1573 kept at Hengrave Hall in Suffolk.

Reward for letting my mistress' blood – 2 shillings.

Galen

Claudius Galenus (AD129–199) was one of the most famous doctors in the ancient world. He studied medicine around the world and in AD161 settled in Rome.

He gave many public lectures on how the body worked and was the first person to realize that human arteries carried blood, not air as most people thought.

He did, however, put forward the incorrect view that good health depended on there being a correct balance of the 'Four Humours' in the body. These were blood, yellow bile, black bile and phlegm. It was to be hundreds of years before this mistake was corrected.

3.3 THE DESERVING POOR AND STURDY BEGGAR

Like all societies the Tudor period had its share of poor people. In fact during this time there was an increase in poor people. There were several reasons for this:

1 Between 1520 and 1580 the population increased by one million. This rapid increase meant that there were more people looking for work and there was not enough food.

2 Cloth making was becoming increasingly important, and more and more land was fenced in so that sheep could graze on it. This was called enclosure. Enclosing land meant that the villagers who farmed it were thrown off and became unemployed.

3 In the mid-sixteenth century prices began to rise. This was called inflation. Wages did not rise in keeping with prices and so many people found it difficult to cope.

Most poor people could not help being poor, but some rich people were frightened when they saw large numbers of poor people. They thought that the poor people might attack them or try to steal their possessions. So poor people were often treated harshly.

But whilst some rich people feared the poor, many considered it their duty to help them. Sources A and D show how the Kytsons at Hengrave Hall went to great lengths to help the local poor.

Source A

These almshouses were built at Hengrave Hall 'for the relief and sustenance of ancient servants of the family or poor persons of the village of Hengrave'.

The worthy and the lazy

Poor people were usually put into one of two categories, the 'deserving poor' and 'sturdy beggars'. The deserving poor were people who could not work because they were too young, too old or too sick. These people were allowed to beg and were often helped out by charity from their local parish.

Sturdy beggars were considered to be much more of a problem. These were people who were fit and well but were out of work. They were not allowed to beg and were considered by many people to be lazy and 'work-shy', though many of them were out of work not by their own fault.

Vagrants

Many sturdy beggars became vagrants – that is, people without a fixed home. Most vagrants made for their local town to look for charity or work. Some of them turned to crime and this frightened the towns-people, who came to see vagrants as a threat. Some people argued that the vagrants were sinners who were out of work because God thought they should be punished. So in some areas vagrants were treated very harshly. Punishments included being branded on the ear, being whipped *until their backs be bloody* and, for persistent beggars, hanging.

However, the government decided that help had to be given to those who could not avoid being poor. In 1572 Parliament passed the Poor Relief Act which raised money from the rich to help pay the deserving poor. But the vagrants were still punished. A law of 1597 said vagrants were to be whipped and sent back to their own county to live in a 'House of Correction'. Persistent vagrants were to be sent abroad to work in the colonies.

Source B

A beggar being whipped through the streets.

Then the great Poor Law Act of 1601 said that parishes had to collect poor rates to help the genuinely poor.

Source C

This story comes from a book printed in 1567 by a magistrate called Thomas Harman. We are not sure whether the story of Nicholas Jennings is true, though Harman seems to have believed it.

Nicholas Jennings was seen begging in London, dressed in rags and covered with blood and dirt. Two apprentices followed him and saw him smear more blood and dirt on himself before carrying on begging. A constable was fetched and Jennings was found to have collected about twenty times the daily wage of a skilled craftsman. They washed him and found there was nothing wrong with him. Luckily for him, he managed to escape.

A few weeks later he was seen begging again and said he was a hat maker who needed money to pay for a room for the night before starting work the next day. He was arrested, whipped, put in the pillory and then into prison. After he promised to stop begging he was released.

Source D

Extracts from the account books of Hengrave Hall showing donations made in 1537 to help the poor.

To old John of the Kitchen at my mistress' command	12 pence
To the collector of the poor in London for 12 weeks at	12 pence a week
To pay for a pair of shoes for Luke the Spaniel boy	13 pence
To help the poor folkes	20 pence

Canting

Tudor beggars used their own 'language' so that they could talk to each other without other people understanding them. They called this 'canting'. A Tudor gentleman called Thomas Dekker made a study of this language. Here are a few of the words they used, and what they meant:

bouse - drink
darkmans - night-time
doxy, mort - woman
duds - clothes
lightmans - daytime
maunderer - rogue

In Tudor times explorers from Europe sailed across the oceans in search of new lands. Their aim was to spread the Christian religion and find new countries with precious metals or spices. These could be captured from the locals or traded in exchange for home-produced goods. Sometimes the explorers just hoped to find short cuts to places with which merchants were already trading, such as China and Asia, which the Europeans called the Indies.

Many of the explorers became famous for their discoveries. For example, Christopher Columbus discovered the Caribbean islands in 1492 and thought that he had found a new route to the Indies, so he called them the 'West Indies'. During this period Europeans discovered not only the West Indies, but also North and South America and a sea route across the tip of Africa to India and the East.

Trading companies

Merchants were keen to exchange goods with the new areas and set up trading companies in England to buy and sell goods overseas. The Muscovy Company brought back furs and timber from Russia and the Baltic, the Turkey Company brought back spices and drugs, the Venetian Company brought back wine and silk, and the great East India Company began to bring spices, silk and jewels from the Far East. Some English merchants became involved in trading people. For example, the Hawkins family in Plymouth sent ships to Africa to fill them with slaves. These were transported to South America where they were sold to people living in the Spanish colonies.

Money from wool

The merchants who traded in the newly-discovered areas were not just buying goods to sell in England. They were also selling home-produced goods. Most common was the woollen cloth made in Norfolk and Yorkshire. This was sold in huge quantities in mainland Europe, but could also be found as far afield as China and India. Some merchants made huge profits. Some, such as Thomas Kytson, invested their money in land, built fine houses and became part of the landed ruling classes of England.

Source A

An English merchant describes the interrogation of a Chinese thief caught trying to steal from an English warehouse in Java at the end of Elizabeth's reign.

...but he would tell us nothing. So I caused him to be burned under the nails of his thumbs, fingers and toes with sharp hot irons. He still made no noise so we burned him in the hands, arms, shoulders and neck. Then we burned him through the hands and with hot irons tore out the flesh and the sinews. After that I caused them to knock the edges of his shin bones with hot searing irons, then to screw iron screws into his arms and finally to break the bones of his fingers and toes with pincers. But still he would not answer our questions. So we put him in irons again and the ants got into his wounds and tormented him.

Finally we tied him to a stake and shot him to death – though it took three bullets to kill him.

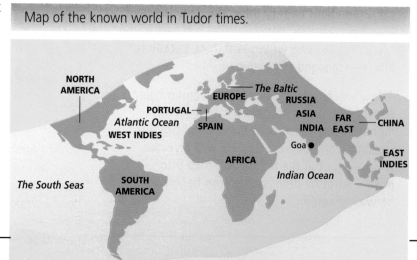

Map of the known world in Tudor times.

NORTH AMERICA
The Baltic
EUROPE
RUSSIA
PORTUGAL
ASIA
Atlantic Ocean
SPAIN
FAR EAST
CHINA
WEST INDIES
INDIA
Goa
EAST INDIES
AFRICA
Indian Ocean
The South Seas
SOUTH AMERICA

Conflict

The great seafarers of Tudor England such as Francis Drake often came into conflict with other European explorers and traders. Their trading was not always peaceful. When relations between England and Spain worsened during the reign of Elizabeth, Drake and others raided Spanish colonies and sank Spanish galleons (after taking off all the treasure, of course!). Throughout this period there were disputes between nations to win control of the new lands being discovered across the seas and to control the trade with those lands.

Source C

A carving from Hengrave Hall. Notice that the figure of Death is wearing a woollen shroud. Queen Elizabeth ordered that everyone should be buried in a woollen shroud. This was a deliberate attempt to boost the sale of woollen cloth in England!

Admiral Sir John Hawkins

Born in Plymouth, John Hawkins (1532-95) was the first Englishman to trade in slaves. He had a successful career in both politics and defence. In 1577, Elizabeth I appointed Hawkins Treasurer of her Navy Board, and he set about his most important task - redesigning the English fleet.

Hawkin's redesigned ships were slimmer, and faster, and much more effective in battle than their clumsy, old-fashioned Spanish counterparts. Hawkins fought alongside Francis Drake and Martin Frobisher against the Spanish. He attacked the heart of the Armada and was rewarded in 1588 with a knighthood from the Queen.

SIR FRANCIS DRAKE

Sir Francis Drake is considered by some historians to have been the greatest of all English seamen. He first became known when he carried out successful attacks on the Spanish in the West Indies between 1567 and 1572. In 1577 he sailed around the world in the *Golden Hind*, capturing gold from Spanish ships along the way. When the Spanish complained, Elizabeth knighted Drake on board his ship. In 1587 he delayed the sailing of the Spanish Armada by carrying out a raid on Cadiz and in 1588 played a major part in defeating the Armada in the English Channel.

When Londoners wanted a bit of fun, they went to the theatre. Rich and poor people flocked to the new theatres around the city. For one penny, people could stand in the **pit** to watch the play. They talked, laughed, shouted and threw rotten eggs at the actors if they did not like what was happening on the stage. They were called the groundlings, and they certainly had fun! People who paid more sat in the covered seats around the stage. Perhaps they saw and heard more of what the actors were saying. Often they were better educated and so they could understand more about the play. The audience could buy food and drink whenever they wanted to during a performance. Many got drunk, and fights broke out. Pick-pockets and all sorts of petty criminals lurked around theatres. Can you think why?

Wandering players and permanent theatres

At first, companies of actors performed plays wherever they found enough people who wanted to watch – for example, in a pub courtyard or a market square. Then, in 1576, an actor called James Burbage built the first permanent theatre, called simply The Theatre, in north London. Others – the Rose, the Swan, the Curtain and the Globe – followed quickly. They all looked more or less the same. A stage jutted out into the pit and the audience watched the action from the front and sides. The middle of the theatre, where the stage was positioned, was open to the sky. Theatres flew a white flag when the weather was good enough for a play to take place. A trumpet was blown when the play was about to start.

Companies of actors performed the plays. There were usually about twelve men and boys in each company, but no women. Boys took the women's and girls' parts.

Plays and playwrights

William Shakespeare (1564–1616) is still the most famous writer of plays in the world. He wrote 38 plays. Some were comedies (such as *A Midsummer Night's Dream*), some were tragedies (such as *Othello*) and some were history plays (such as *Richard III*). Christopher Marlowe (see unit 3.6) was Shakespeare's closest rival as a playwright and poet. He was killed in a pub fight when he was 29 years old. Most playwrights and actors had an important person as their **patron** and called their company after him. Shakespeare belonged to the Lord Chamberlain's Men, and with them he acted plays watched by Elizabeth I.

Opposition to the theatre

Source A

Part of a sermon preached by a Puritan, John Stockwood, in London in 1578.

Will not a filthy play, with the blast of a trumpet, call 1000 to watch it, whilst an hour's tolling of the bell will call only 100 to church to hear the sermon?

Source B

This was written by another Puritan, in a book called *A Second and Third Blast of Retreat from Plays and Theatres* in 1580.

Whosoever shall visit the chapel of Satan, I mean the theatre, shall find many young ruffians, all past shame.

Source C

An extract from the diary of Philip Henslowe, a theatre manager. Henslowe kept a diary at the end of the 1500s.

Three companies of players will be allowed to act their plays in the Globe, the Fortune and the Curtain. However, if more than thirty people a week die of the plague in the City of London then these theatres will be closed until the figure is back down to thirty a week.

William Shakespeare

William Shakespeare is England's most famous playwright. He was born in 1564 in Stratford-upon-Avon, and is thought to have attended the local grammar school. In 1582 he married Anne Hathaway, the daughter of a local farmer, and they had two daughters and one son.

In 1588 Shakespeare moved to London and within a few years, gained a reputation as an actor and playwright. His plays were performed for both Elizabeth I and James I. In his later years he returned to Stratford, where he died in 1616. He was buried in the local church.

3.6 CHRISTOPHER MARLOWE: A MURDER MYSTERY?

What happened?

On the morning of 30 May 1593, four men, Ingram Frizer, Nicholas Skeres, Robert Poley and Christopher Marlowe, met at a house in Deptford, London. No one knows what they spent the morning discussing at this quiet private meeting. Widow Eleanor Bull, who owned the house, took them lunch and afterwards the four men walked and talked in the garden. At about six o'clock in the evening, the men came in from the garden and ate supper. Suddenly a row flared up. It was about the bill, or 'reckoning'. Marlowe snatched Frizer's dagger and hit him several times on the head with its handle. Frizer tried to get the dagger off Marlowe. Somehow, in the struggle, the dagger blade was thrust into Christopher Marlowe's right eye and he died instantly. Frizer was arrested but later acquitted because it was said he was acting in self-defence.

Some experts say this is a portrait of Christopher Marlowe. It hangs in Corpus Christi College, Cambridge, where he was a student. It was painted in 1585, when he was 21 years old.

Source A

Our knowledge of events on that May evening comes from the coroner's inquest. But the only people giving evidence who really knew what happened were Ingram Frizer, Nicholas Skeres and Robert Poley. Can we trust their version of events?

The Deptford Four

Robert Poley and Nicholas Skeres were involved in **intelligence work** for the government. Ingram Frizer was servant to Thomas Walsingham, who was employed in secret work by his cousin Francis, the Queen's spymaster (Source C). Christopher Marlowe began working as a government agent while he was at Cambridge University. He was sent to France to spy on English Catholics. The Privy Council wrote to the university saying that Marlowe had *done Her Majesty great service* and was to be rewarded for his *faithful dealing*.

Was Marlowe's killing more than just a pub brawl?

Source B

A description of Christopher Marlowe from a book called *The Reckoning*, written in 1992 by Charles Nicholl.

He is remembered not just as a writer, but as someone who did not believe in the existence of God, a man who swore, was a homosexual, lived fast and died young.

An unbeliever?

An atheist is someone who doesn't believe that God exists. To be an atheist in Elizabethan days was dangerous. The Elizabethan Church and the state were so closely linked that anyone who denied the existence of God was said to be an enemy of the state.

Christopher Marlowe was an atheist. On 18 May, when he was staying with Thomas Walsingham, he was summoned to appear before the Privy Council. Some atheistic writings, said to be by Marlowe, had been found. Marlowe was allowed to go free provided he reported to the Privy Council every day while investigations proceeded. On 30 May the Council received a report from their agent, Richard Baines (Source D). If Marlowe was guilty as Baines said, he would have been executed after days of torture and interrogation. Who knows what Marlowe might have said while being interrogated? Baines' report said Marlowe met with people in high places who shared his views. Under torture, Marlowe might have incriminated anybody. Then on the evening of 30 May 1593 he died in a brawl.

The Shakespeare connection

But can we be certain that Marlowe was murdered? Marlowe wrote brilliant plays and poems. He worked with Shakespeare at the Shoreditch theatre and some people believe he recruited Shakespeare into the secret service. In the 1950s a Canadian journalist, Calvin Hoffman, developed the theory that Marlowe's death had been staged to protect people like Walsingham. Marlowe, so Hoffman says, lived on and wrote some of the plays that nearly everyone says were written by William Shakespeare.

Source C

This portrait of Queen Elizabeth's spymaster, Francis Walsingham, was painted in 1585. He was Secretary of State and set up England's secret service. It became the most feared network of spies in Europe.

Source D

Part of the report from Richard Baines to the Privy Council in May 1593, stating what Christopher Marlowe was supposed to have said. The report listed one and a half pages of similar accusations.

That Christ was illegitimate and Mary his mother dishonest ... that Christ deserved better to die than Barabas and that Jews made a good choice ... if there be a God or any religion it is the Catholics'.

Shakespeare or Marlowe?

When Marlowe wasn't getting himself involved in devious spying or brawls in taverns, he was actually a very talented writer! He had an excellent education and his most famous play, *Dr. Faustus,* tells the chilling story of a man who sold his soul to the devil. His style of writing, in poem form, was copied by Shakespeare and this has encouraged some experts to think that some of Shakespeare's plays might actually have been written by Marlowe himself. A more extreme view is that Marlowe did not die in the tavern brawl, but instead took on a new identity – William Shakespeare!

4.1 RELIGION IN THE SEVENTEENTH CENTURY

The seventeenth century was an exciting time. There were many different ideas about how God should be worshipped. Some members of the Church of England, called Puritans, wanted a far simpler type of service than was normal in the Church of England. This led to many arguments inside the Church. Others became **Dissenters** and experimented with different kinds of Church organisation and different ways of worshipping.

As you have read, it was Henry VIII who began setting up the Church of England, which is now often called the Anglican Church. From that time onwards it was not really safe to be a Catholic. But many Catholics kept up their religion secretly all through the sixteenth and seventeenth centuries.

Very few people admitted to not believing in the Christian God. Belief in a God was still a central part of most people's lives, no matter how they thought they should worship.

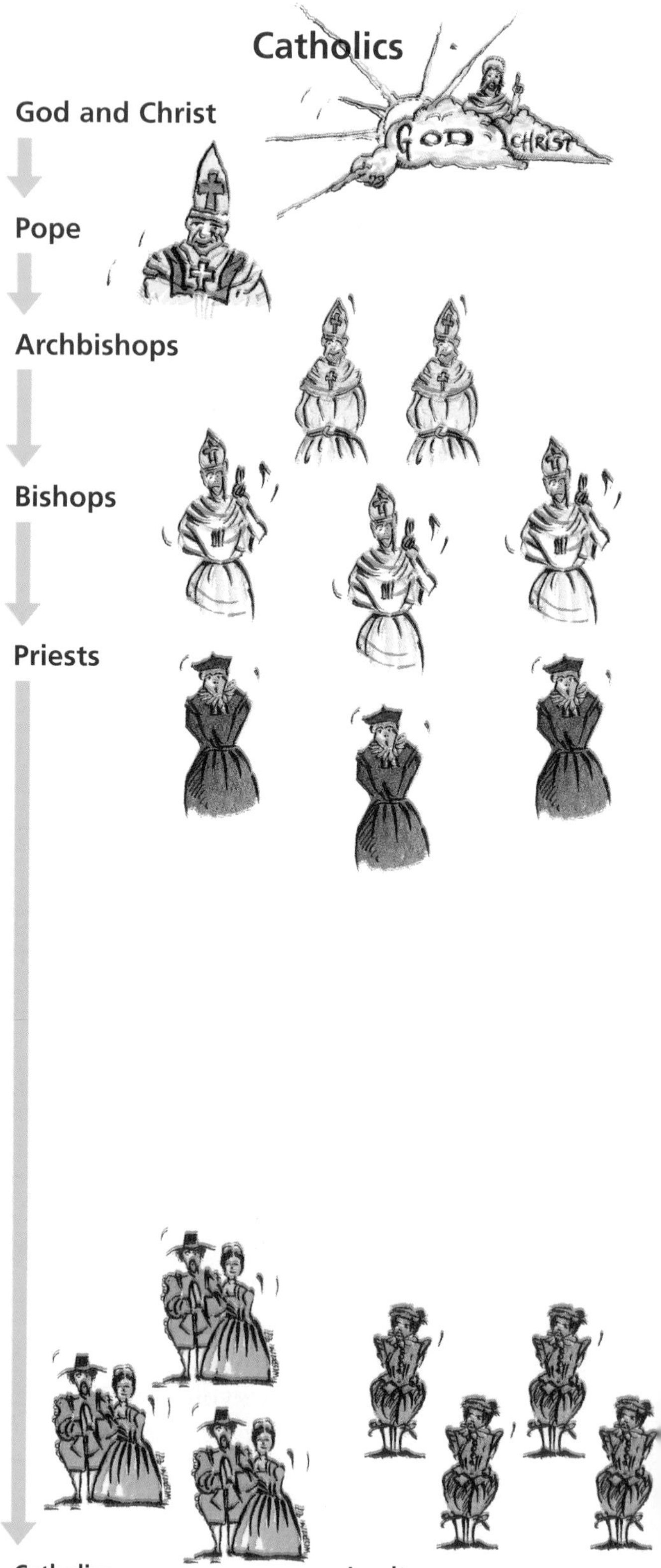
Catholics
God and Christ
GOD
CHRIST
Pope
Archbishops
Bishops
Priests

Catholics

People who followed the teachings of the Roman Catholic Church.

Jesuits

Catholic priests who were full of enthusiasm in following Catholic teachings and teaching others to do so.

Religious groups in the seventeenth century.

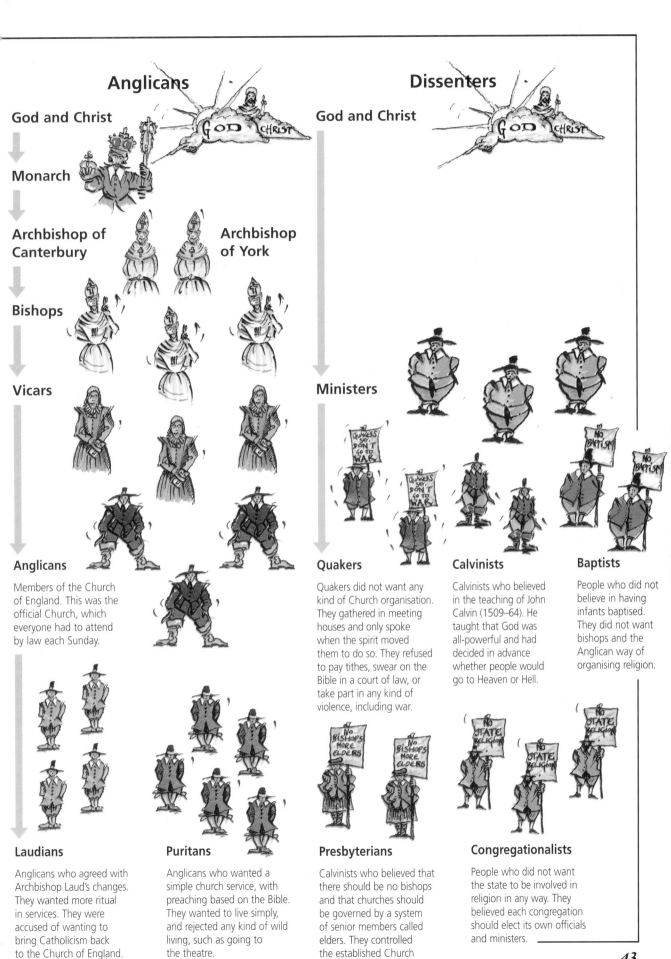

Anglicans

God and Christ

Monarch

Archbishop of Canterbury　　**Archbishop of York**

Bishops

Vicars

Anglicans

Members of the Church of England. This was the official Church, which everyone had to attend by law each Sunday.

Laudians

Anglicans who agreed with Archbishop Laud's changes. They wanted more ritual in services. They were accused of wanting to bring Catholicism back to the Church of England.

Puritans

Anglicans who wanted a simple church service, with preaching based on the Bible. They wanted to live simply, and rejected any kind of wild living, such as going to the theatre.

Dissenters

God and Christ

Ministers

Quakers

Quakers did not want any kind of Church organisation. They gathered in meeting houses and only spoke when the spirit moved them to do so. They refused to pay tithes, swear on the Bible in a court of law, or take part in any kind of violence, including war.

Calvinists

Calvinists who believed in the teaching of John Calvin (1509–64). He taught that God was all-powerful and had decided in advance whether people would go to Heaven or Hell.

Baptists

People who did not believe in having infants baptised. They did not want bishops and the Anglican way of organising religion.

Presbyterians

Calvinists who believed that there should be no bishops and that churches should be governed by a system of senior members called elders. They controlled the established Church in Scotland.

Congregationalists

People who did not want the state to be involved in religion in any way. They believed each congregation should elect its own officials and ministers.

43

Both Catholics and Puritans had high hopes of James I, who succeeded Queen Elizabeth in 1603. The Catholics remembered that his mother, Mary, Queen of Scots, had been a sincere Catholic all her life. Surely he would allow Catholics to worship in their own way? The Puritans remembered that James had been brought up as a Calvinist by Scottish lords, who took him away from the influence of his mother when he was a baby. They presumed that he would alter Church of England ceremonies to make them less like Catholic ones. But neither Catholics nor Puritans were pleased by what James did.

Source A

This picture of James with his mother Mary, Queen of Scots, was painted in 1583. James had not seen his mother since he was a baby, and so they could not have sat together to have their portraits painted.

The Hampton Court Conference, 1604

James I called the Anglican bishops and the Puritans to a conference. He hoped to make peace between them. James agreed to the Puritans' demands that women should not be allowed to baptise, that there should be more preaching in church and that the number of parishes that priests could work in should be reduced. But when the Puritans asked for bishops to be abolished and for clergymen to be elected, James was angry. The Puritans were trying to take control of the Church away from the ruling classes. The conference ended with the Puritans dissatisfied and James and his bishops angry.

The King James Bible, 1611

At the conference King James ordered a new translation of the Bible. This was in English, not Latin, and was easy to understand. With this new Bible, people understood Christianity for themselves without having everything explained by a priest. But this brought more problems for the Church of England. People began to make up their own minds about what they believed. Some left the Anglican Church and joined other Christian groups. So the numbers of Dissenters in the country grew.

In 1625 James died and was followed by his son, Charles I, who had been an Anglican all his life.

Source B

Remarks made by James I at the Hampton Court Conference in 1604.

I shall make them [the Puritans] conform or I will harry them out of the land, or else do worse.

No bishops, no king!

Source C

In 1637 Archbishop Laud and the Star Chamber sentenced three Puritans to have their ears cut off for criticising the Church. One of the Puritans, William Prynne, is holding his head where his ears once were. The ears are on the plate in front of Laud.

Source D

Part of a speech made by James I to Parliament in 1609 in which he describes the Divine Right of Kings. Later, his son Charles I said that a version of the Divine Right of Kings had to be read out in every church at least four times a year.

The state of monarchy is the supremest thing upon earth. Kings are not only God's lieutenants upon earth, and sit upon God's throne, but even by God himself they are called gods. They are judges over all their subjects and accountable to none but God.

Archbishop Laud, Puritans and Anglicans

In the 1630s Charles I and William Laud, the Archbishop of Canterbury (1578–1645), began to make changes to the Church of England. He said that churches could be decorated and have stained-glass windows. The communion table had to be moved to the east end of the church and have rails put round it. People bowed their heads when they passed it, like in Catholic churches. The Puritans were alarmed. Charles was married to Henrietta Maria, a Catholic. She had her own Catholic chapel in the royal palace. Was Charles a Catholic too? Was he encouraging Laud to bring back the Catholic Church? Many Puritans followed the example of the Pilgrim Fathers (see Unit 4.4) and emigrated to America. They did not want to live in a country with a Catholic religion.

Laud hated the Puritans, with their plain clothes, plain churches and long sermons. He thought people would worship better if they had beautiful things in their churches. He did his best to ban Puritan books and imprison Puritan writers and preachers.

Laud's changes made Protestants very angry. When Parliament met in 1640, it began attacking Laud's religious politics. These quarrels would later erupt into bloody civil war.

William Laud

Laud was Archbishop of Canterbury during the reign of Charles I but was a victim of the dispute between Charles and Parliament in the 1640s. Laud was born in 1537, in Reading, Berkshire and attended Oxford University. In 1601 he was ordained as a priest and his talents brought him regular promotion. In 1611 he was made the King's Chaplain and was Bishop of St Andrews, Bath and Wells and finally London before he was made Archbishop of Canterbury in 1623.

He was a strong opponent of the Puritan ideas that worship should be plain, with little music or colour. His opponents thought that what he really wanted was to restore the Catholic religion to England.

In 1637 Laud, with the support of King Charles, tried to introduce the English Prayer Book into Scotland. There were riots against the English, finally resulting in a war between England and Scotland. Charles I was forced to ask Parliament for help, and one of its conditions was that Laud should go. He was found guilty on a charge of treason and beheaded in 1645.

Source A

*my lord out of the loue i beare ~~vnto~~ To some of youer freindz
I haue a caer of youer preseruacion therfor i would...
aduyse yowe as yoube Tender youer Lyf To deuys some
epscuse To shift of youer aHendaunce at THis parleament*

This is part of the letter supposed to have been written by Francis Tresham to his brother-in-law, Lord Monteagle. It says: *My Lord out of the love I bear to some of your friends I have a care of your preservation therefore I would advise you as you tender your life to devise some excuse to shift of your attendance at this parliament.* Some historians say it is a fake.

Catholics hoped for much from James. However, his government and parliaments were Protestant. So Catholics grew angry and disappointed at what they saw as a lack of progress. In November 1605, Robert Cecil, Earl of Salisbury and King James' chief minister, revealed that a terrible plot had been uncovered. A group of Catholics had tried to blow up the Houses of Parliament. How had this come about?

The plan

On 5 November James was due to attend the state opening of Parliament. Robert Cecil explained that a desperate group of Catholics, well-known troublemakers, had planned to take advantage of the situation and blow King, Lords and Commons sky high. The plotters, led by Robert Catesby and funded by Francis Tresham, first tried to tunnel under the House of Lords from a nearby house. This failed. Then, in February 1605, another plotter, Thomas Percy, rented a cellar right underneath the House of Lords and hid 36 barrels of gunpowder there. The plotters waited for the opening of Parliament. For seven months the gunpowder lay undiscovered.

The arrest

In October, Francis Tresham decided to warn his brother-in-law, Lord Monteagle. He sent him a letter telling him not to go to the state opening of Parliament on 5 November. Monteagle sent the letter straight to Cecil. On the night of 4 November, Cecil ordered a search of the cellars under the Parliament building. There guards found the gunpowder and Guy Fawkes. Fawkes was a Yorkshire Catholic who had served with the Spanish army. He was arrested and tortured, and made a full confession.

Most of the plotters were tracked down to Holbeache House in Staffordshire, where they were surrounded by soldiers. Catesby and Percy were shot. Two others died in the struggle and the rest were taken to London. A special committee was set up to decide what to do with the plotters. It was decided they should be hanged, drawn and quartered.

All over England Protestants lit bonfires to celebrate the failure of the Gunpowder Plot. More people turned against the Catholics. Parliament passed laws forbidding Catholics to hold important jobs in the government. They were watched by government spies and over 5000 were arrested. It was not an easy time to be a Catholic.

Source B

An early seventeenth-century print of the executions of the gunpowder plotters.

Guy Fawkes

Guy Fawkes was born in York in 1570. He was born a Protestant, but his mother remarried a recusant, which meant that Guy had a lot of contact with Catholicism from an early age. He went to school with Catholics, including the Wright brothers who were later to be involved in the Gunpowder plot.

Guy Fawkes later converted to Catholicism, and enlisted in the Spanish army where he could practise his religion openly. There he changed his name to Guido, the Spanish form of Guy. Guy believed that, given the opportunity, English Catholics would rise up and rid the country of their Protestant king. He was wrong.

When Fawkes was arrested around midnight on 4 November 1605 he used the false name 'John Johnson'. Fuses and kindling were found in his pocket. He was executed later the same year.

Unanswered questions

The story of the Gunpowder Plot which you have just read is the story told by Robert Cecil. Many historians question Cecil's version of the 'facts'. They say there are too many unanswered questions:

- Why was the tunnel that was dug between a neighbouring house and Parliament not shown to anyone?
- Why was Thomas Percy, a discontented Catholic well known to Cecil's spies, allowed to rent a cellar under the Houses of Parliament?
- How did the plotters manage to buy so much gunpowder when its sale was controlled by the government?
- Cecil learned of the 'plot' in October; why did he wait until 4 November before ordering Parliament's cellars to be searched?
- Did Tresham really write the warning letter? Some handwriting experts think Cecil did.
- Were Catesby and Percy shot to stop them talking?
- Why did the man who killed them receive two shillings a day for the rest of his life?
- Why was Lord Monteagle granted a huge pension afterwards?

4.4 PURITANS PROTEST: THE PILGRIM FATHERS, 1620

Decisions

The reign of James I was a difficult time for Puritans. They knew that James I did not approve of them and that they would be better off in a different country. So many of them fled to Holland.

The truce which enabled them to stay there was due to run out in 1621. Where could the English Puritans go? They desperately wanted to worship God in their own way and live simple, worthy lives, free from outside interference. They knew that there was already one English colony on the Atlantic coast of North America. Jamestown, in Virginia, had been founded in 1607 and seemed successful. Could they set up a new colony themselves?

The journey

The English Puritans returned to England to look for a ship and a crew willing to take them across the Atlantic. The *Mayflower*, a ship 90 feet long and 20 feet wide, set sail for America with 100 'Pilgrims' and twenty-five crew in October 1620. Everything they thought they would need to start a new colony was packed in the hold. Conditions were bad: crammed between decks with no portholes, the Pilgrims suffered sea-sickness and dysentery. They washed in sea water and just a fortnight into the two-month crossing they ran out of fresh food. One man died and a baby, christened Oceanus, was born. The ship's timbers leaked and Atlantic storms tore the sails and rigging. Finally, on 20 December 1620, the *Mayflower* anchored in the peace and calm of Cape Cod, off the coast of North America.

Source A

This is part of an agreement, called the Mayflower Compact, which was made on board the *Mayflower*. It was signed by the heads of all forty-one families on board. Once on dry land, they agreed to elect a governor and a court which would make all the laws for the new settlement.

We, whose names are underwritten, the loyal subjects of our dread sovereign Lord, King James, do combine ourselves into a civil body politic [government] for our better ordering and preservation.

Spanish, French and English settlement in America by 1700.

Francis Eaton

Francis Eaton was one of the original Puritans to go to America on the *Mayflower* in October, 1620. He was born in September 1596 in Bristol, and worked as a carpenter. Francis was 24 when he set sail on the *Mayflower* with his first wife, Sarah, and their new-born son, Samuel. Sadly, Sarah did not survive the first winter. Francis returned to Plymouth, where he died in 1633 from an unknown disease that claimed many other *Mayflower* passengers that year.

Early years

Once they had landed, the Pilgrims needed to find a safe site for a settlement. They had to cut down trees for timber to build their homes, and clear land to plant the seeds they had brought with them. The first year was terrible. Fifty-one settlers died from disease or lack of food. Their crops failed. Then a Native American Indian tribe, the Wampanoag, made a peace treaty with them. The Indians taught the settlers how to hunt and grow crops in the Indian way. The Pilgrims learned how to bury fish in the ground as fertiliser. They planted corn, pumpkins and beans. It all worked. The harvest in the autumn of 1621 was a good one. The settlers celebrated with the Indians for three days: they ate roast turkey and goose and thanked God for what had happened.

Americans still celebrate the success of the Pilgrim Fathers. The fourth Thursday in November is Thanksgiving Day in the USA, when Americans remember the Pilgrim Fathers, and the Native American Indians who helped them. Families and friends gather for a meal of roast turkey and pumpkin pie.

James VI of Scotland

James Stuart became James VI of Scotland when he was a baby. He had a lonely childhood. Plots surrounded him as the Scottish nobles and clergy battled over who would influence the young ruler. James learned quickly. He brought peace to the Highlands by turning his enemies against one another when the **clan** chiefs threatened to rebel. He set up a system of justice for the whole of Scotland. He did what he could to make the country prosperous by encouraging trade and industry.

This picture of James I was painted by an artist at the time.

He managed to control the Church, too. Scotland had a **Presbyterian** Church, or Kirk. Each congregation chose its own minister, and all the ministers and elected members of the Kirk met every year in a General Assembly. In spite of opposition from the General Assembly, James governed the Kirk and insisted that bishops, appointed by him, kept their jobs.

James I, King of England

In March 1603 Elizabeth I of England was dying. Her ministers tried to persuade her to say who should inherit her throne. Finally she murmured, *Who should that be but our cousin of Scotland?* The English peers and Privy Council had backed James' claim to the throne. Most of his new subjects seemed satisfied, too, because he was a Protestant and the great-grandson of Henry VIII's elder sister. James was delighted with his new inheritance. He made his way south from Edinburgh, giving rewards to everyone who entertained him and his followers. He spent two nights at Hinchingbrooke in Huntingdon, owned by Sir Oliver Cromwell. Loaded down with gifts from the Cromwell family on that day in 1603, James could never have guessed that forty-six years later his own son Charles would be executed and that the nephew of this Sir Oliver would be one of the men responsible for putting him to death.

Source B

A description of James written by Sir Anthony Weldon in 1650 in his book *The Court and Character of James I*.

He was fat. His eyes were large, ever rolling after any stranger that came into his presence. His tongue was too large for his mouth. His drink came out of each side of his mouth and dribbled back into the cup. He never washed his hands. He was crafty and cunning in small things but a fool in important matters.

James and Parliament

During his reign, James I had trouble with his parliaments, but the trouble was not all of his own making. Elizabeth I had left behind debts of around £300,000. Parliament, out of respect for her age, had not pushed for the changes it wanted.

James started out by choosing some ministers the Commons disliked. His favourite was George Villiers, who became Duke of Buckingham in 1623. James loaded him with honours and wealth, and Parliament hated him. This showed how little James understood the English system. Monarchs usually took the advice of their most important subjects.

James needed money. He had to pay off Elizabeth's debts, and he also had a large family to keep. On top of this, being a monarch was more expensive than in Elizabeth's day. Prices were rising fast and James' income bought less. Parliament tried to control James by keeping him short of money. In 1610, for example, it refused him extra income because it said he was asking for too much. James began selling **peerages** at £1000 a time and borrowing from the London banks. He raised taxes on imported goods in order to increase his income.

Members of Parliament believed that the King should not raise taxes without their agreement. They grew angry when he lectured them on the Divine Right of Kings. James thought they were meddlers who were trying to interfere with the way he wanted to rule the country. This was a bad mistake. He was upsetting the people he had to work with if he was going to run the country well. However, most of them, the lords, gentry, clergy and Members of Parliament, were basically loyal to the Crown and to James.

Source C

A description of James by a modern historian, Maurice Ashley. He wrote this in *England in the Seventeenth Century* in 1952.

King James I was a clever and learned man – far from the slobbering *quibbler* he has sometimes been made out. His defects were vanity and a softness in his nature, shown by his habit of lecturing people at one moment and giving way to them at another, and a liking for worthless favourites.

Source D

From a letter written by James I to the Spanish ambassador in 1621.

The House of Commons is like a body without a head. The members give their opinions noisily. I am surprised English kings ever allowed such a place to exist.

Sir Anthony Weldon

Anthony Weldon came from a family with a wide experience of service to the royal family. His father, uncle and two sons all held positions in the royal courts of Elizabeth I, James I and Charles I. Weldon was knighted in 1617 and, in the same year, accompanied James I on a royal visit to Scotland. He is said to have been dismissed, also in the same year, because James discovered that he had written a book criticising Scotland.

During the Civil War Weldon fought on the side of Parliament, which voted him a large sum of money for his efforts in keeping the County of Kent loyal to its cause. Towards the end of his life Weldon wrote a book called *The Court and Character of James I*. This was really nothing more than a collection of scandalous gossip about James. It contains some personal reminiscences but has very little in it which can be confirmed as historical fact.

Charles became king in 1625 when his father, James I, died. Charles was a big spender. Not only did he spend money on his family, his favourites and his friends, but he needed to pay for wars against France and Spain. Prices had risen, too, and so everything was more expensive. Charles, like his father, had to ask Parliament for taxes. The problem was that every time Parliament met, it discussed its complaints and offered advice to the King before agreeing to raise any money. This irritated, and sometimes angered, Charles.

What did Parliament want?

Parliament could not control the King's policies, but MPs did expect Charles to listen to them and to take notice of their worries and complaints. Charles, on the other hand, believed in his divine right to rule. He believed he could rule without Parliament if he wanted to.

Was Ship Money fair?

In 1628 MPs presented Charles with a 'Petition of Right'. This said that no taxes should be collected without Parliament's permission. Charles had had enough. He decided to see if he could manage without Parliament. He knew he could collect a tax called 'Ship Money' without Parliament's consent. This was a tax collected in coastal counties in wartime. It was used to build and maintain fighting ships. Charles decided to collect this tax every year, even though there was no war on.

This ship, the *Sovereign of the Seas*, was paid for by Ship Money and launched in 1637.

Source A

This is what a Puritan, Sir Simonds d'Ewes, wrote about Ship Money at the time.

In 1635 all the sheriffs in the land were told to levy great sums of money. This was under the pretence of providing ships for the defence of the kingdom. But we were at peace with all the world and the fleet was strong. If the King could levy what taxes he liked on his subjects and then imprison them when they refused to pay, then all our liberties were utterly ruined.

In 1635 he extended it to include inland counties as well. It looked as though Charles would be able to rule without Parliament – as long as he did not have to pay for an expensive war.

John Hampden, a rich country gentleman, believed Ship Money was illegal and refused to pay it. He was brought to court and, after a long trial, ordered to pay. But Hampden knew that nearly half of the judges who tried his case agreed with him, and so did most MPs and gentry.

Source B

Was Charles I a secret Catholic?

Charles I was the first monarch to be born and brought up within the Protestant Church of England. Yet he had a Catholic wife and some Puritans believed he was a secret Catholic. They believed Archbishop Laud's changes were just one step on the way to turning England Catholic again.

The Arch-Prelate of St Andrewes in Scotland reading the new Service-booke in his pontificall asaulted by men & Women, with Crickets stooles Stickes and Stones

A cartoon from the time, showing a riot in a Scottish church in 1637.

Scotland: Charles' big mistake

Charles wanted all his subjects to worship God in much the same way. In 1637 he ordered the Scottish Presbyterian Church to use the same prayer book as the Church of England. Charles and Laud discussed the introduction of the new prayer book with the Scottish bishops, but not with the General Assembly of the Kirk. Riots broke out during church services in Edinburgh. In 1638 a group of important Scots drew up the National Covenant, which thousands of people signed. These **Covenanters** vowed to defend their Kirk (Church) against the King and his bishops. They formed an army and marched into England. Charles was faced with what he had most dreaded: an expensive war. Could he still manage without Parliament? The only army Charles could put together was far too weak to defeat the Covenanters. In May 1640 he was forced to call Parliament to ask for money to raise an army.

Charles knew that recalling Parliament was likely to cause him great difficulties. He had ruled without Parliament for eleven years and the new MPs were bound to complain about his behaviour. This is exactly what happened; the new Parliament refused to help Charles until he agreed to let it have more say in how the country was run. Charles was so angry that he dismissed the Parliament after just three weeks!

But Charles still had to deal with the invading Scots. Without money from Parliament he could not raise an army large enough to defeat them. So he negotiated a humiliating treaty with the Scots, giving into their demands and agreeing to pay their expenses. Of course, he did not have the money to do so. So in November it was back to Parliament again!

John Hampden

Known as the 'Father of the People' because of his opposition to the Ship Money tax, John Hampden (1594–1643) was a leading figure in the resistance to the rule of Charles I. As a result of his rebelliousness, John was one of the five Members of Parliament whom Charles tried to arrest in 1642 (see page 55). When the Civil War broke out, John commanded a Parliamentarian foot regiment, but he was mortally wounded in the Battle of Charlgrove Field.

November 1640: Parliament meets again

In November 1640 the new parliament met. Unlike the last parliament, this one was to last, on and off, for twenty years and was known as the 'Long Parliament'. But in November 1640 no one realised how successful Parliament would be in its struggle with the King.

The new MPs were furious at the way Charles had been running the country, and in particular at the way Parliament had been treated. Led by John Pym (1584–1643), they said that their **grievances** had to be settled before any taxes would be granted to the King. Charles was desperate. He had to accept Parliament's demands. He agreed that the ways in which he had raised money in the past eleven years were illegal. He agreed that Parliament would meet every three years. He agreed to abandon the changes Archbishop Laud had brought to the Church. He even allowed Laud to be imprisoned without trial and his closest adviser, the Earl of Strafford, to be executed on the orders of Parliament. John Pym and the Parliamentarians seemed to have won control over the King, but Charles did not give up easily.

Ireland

In 1640 Irish Catholics, frightened that the English Protestant Parliament would pass anti-Catholic laws, rebelled and killed around 3000 Protestants in Ulster. Charles hoped that the country would unite against the Irish rebels and that his quarrel with Parliament would be forgotten. The King asked for money to raise an army to put down this rebellion. But Parliament was afraid that Charles would use this army against his opponents in England. Pym demanded that Parliament should control any army sent to Ireland. Charles had had enough. He decided to get rid of Pym.

Source D

This is a scene from the film *Cromwell*. Charles is looking for the five MPs.

John Pym

Pym (1584–1643) was a leading parliamentarian who played a major part in opposing Charles I in the years leading up to the Civil War.

He was born in Brymore in Somerset and became an MP in 1614. He helped draw up the Petition of Right in 1628 and was one of the five Members of Parliament whom Charles tried to arrest in 1642. He died in London during the Civil War.

'The birds are flown'

Charles decided to go to Parliament and arrest John Pym and four other leading MPs. He knew that he could be accused of using force against an elected Parliament but was prepared to take this risk. On 4 January 1642 Charles burst into the House of Commons with armed men. The five members had been tipped off beforehand and had fled. Charles was very angry. He said to the Speaker, *Since I see all the birds are flown, I expect you to send them to me as soon as they return.* The Speaker refused to be bullied by the King, saying *I have neither eyes to see nor tongue to speak in this place, except as the House is pleased to direct me.* Charles was furious, especially as Parliament now knew he could not be trusted. Charles decided that the only way to maintain his authority was to defeat Parliament and its supporters in battle. On 22 August at Nottingham he appealed for supporters to join him. In response Parliament raised its own army. The Civil War had begun.

Brother against brother

The Civil War broke out because the King and Parliament had become so suspicious of each other that they could not work together. Now the matter had to be settled by fighting. But who was going to fight on each side?

Strong supporters of the King joined the Royalists (or 'Cavaliers'). This included most of the House of Lords, members of the Anglican Church and major landowners. Parliament's side (the 'Roundheads') was supported by MPs, and most merchants, manufacturers and Puritans. But there were many exceptions to this. Sometimes lifelong friends found themselves on different sides. Even brothers ended up fighting against each other in battles. Most ordinary people had little to do with the fighting. When the war came close to their homes, they might end up fighting for whichever side their local lord supported. Otherwise they kept out of the way.

The King had many advantages. He was the rightful ruler, and many people did not want to fight him. He had money, because many wealthy men and landowners were on his side. He had one simple aim, which was to capture London: this, he thought, would end all opposition. Most Parliamentarians did not like fighting their own king. They simply wanted him to agree to some of their demands.

The fighting

Warfare in the seventeenth century was very different from the kind of wars fought today.

At the Battle of the Somme in World War 1 (1916) the British army suffered 60,000 casualties on the first day. At the first major battle of the Civil War, Edgehill in October 1642, there were only 28,000 soldiers in total and only a few thousand casualties.

The reason for the small number of casualties was that the fighting was done hand to hand using swords and a long spear, known as a pike. Soldiers also used muskets and cannon, but these were nowhere near as effective as the weapons used today. They also sometimes caused confusion, as you can see in Source E.

Source E

Edmund Ludlow, a Parliamentarian soldier and MP, tells the story of how his side fired on its own soldiers at the Battle of Edgehill in October 1642.

We sent a servant to load one of the cannon. He had just done this when a group of horsemen came up from the enemy's side of the field. We fired at them, but only wounded one man in the hand because the cannon was overloaded and on too high ground. Just as well, for they were from our own side! They had charged into the enemy ranks to put the enemy's cannon out of action and we had fired upon them on their way back.

The Civil War lasted until 1646 when Charles surrendered to the Scottish army. The Scots then sold him to the English Parliament. Why did the Parliamentarians win?

The generals

Generals are important because they work out the tactics to be used during battles and they inspire their troops to fight well and bravely. One of the most important generals on the Royalist side was Prince Rupert of the Rhine (1618–92), who was King Charles' nephew. He was brave and romantic, but he often made decisions without thinking them through and was not always in full control of his men. The Puritan Oliver Cromwell became the most important Parliamentarian general. His well thought-out tactics made him famous. His troops were always well disciplined and, with Thomas Fairfax, he formed the New Model Army in 1645.

The officers

Some officers on the Parliamentarian side were MPs who did not really want to defeat the King in battle. Parliament wanted to get these faint-hearted MPs out of the army. In 1645 Parliament passed a 'Self-Denying Ordinance'. This said that no member of the Lords or Commons could be an army officer. The only exception was Oliver Cromwell.

Thomas Fairfax

Fairfax (1612–71) was the Commander in Chief of Parliament's troops in the Civil War, but by 1660 he had decided that monarchy should be restored.

The major battles of the Civil War and the outcomes.

Royalists

Parliamentarians

Edgehill October 1642	Indecisive
Newbury September 1643	Indecisive
Marston Moor July 1644	Victory for Parliament and Scots
Naseby June 1645	Victory for Parliament
Preston August 1648	Parliament smashes Royalists and Scots

The New Model Army

Oliver Cromwell and Sir Thomas Fairfax (1612–71), who had been made a general by Parliament, turned their army into an efficient fighting force with a Puritan religious zeal. The officers were trained and the soldiers were drilled. They were well equipped, well fed and paid. The Royalists joked about this new army and called it the New Noddle Army. But in June 1645 it defeated them decisively at Naseby, the last major battle of the war.

Allies

Allies are important in any war. At first, Charles thought other kings in Europe would send troops and money to support him. Not one monarch did. Charles made peace in Ireland and so his army there came back to fight in England.

In 1643 John Pym made an offer to the Scots. If Parliament won it would set up a Presbyterian Church in England, like the one in Scotland. The Scots had not forgotten how Charles had tried to force them to use the English prayer book. So they sent 20,000 men to fight on Parliament's side. They helped defeat the Royalists at Marston Moor in July 1644 and so won control of the North of England. By the time the Scots decided to change sides (see page 58), the New Model Army was fighting well. Scots and Royalists were badly defeated at Preston in the 'Second Civil War' in 1648.

Money

Wars cost money. Charles had many very wealthy supporters and could have funded a short war easily. But there was no quick victory for him and his supporters. The Parliamentarians, on the other hand, controlled London with its rich merchants. The Parliamentarians were also much more efficient than the Royalists at collecting taxes from the areas they controlled. The King could not afford to raise another army after many of his men were killed at Naseby in 1645.

A modern painting of a Royalist charge at the Battle of Edgehill in 1642.

Source A

In 1646 Charles surrendered to the Scots. They tried, and failed, to make a deal with him and so in February 1647 they handed him over to Parliament. Parliament started to negotiate with Charles. This is what it had always wanted. At this stage there was no question of killing him.

The war was over, so Parliament ordered its army to disband. But the soldiers were owed many months' pay and refused to go home. The situation looked serious. Cromwell and Fairfax (who agreed with the troops) acted quickly. The King was taken to Newmarket, where he was now a prisoner of the army, not Parliament. Army officers began negotiating with him. They also said that the Commons should be **purged** of MPs who disagreed with them.

Was the King a double dealer?

Cromwell began trying to make a deal with Charles. But just when they seemed to be reaching an agreement, Cromwell discovered that Charles had been negotiating secretly with the Scots. To make matters worse, Charles escaped from the army and fled to the Isle of Wight. There he signed an alliance with the Scots. They agreed that the Scots would invade England and fight for Charles. In return he would set up an English Presbyterian Church. However, Royalists and Scots were wiped out by the New Model Army at Preston in August 1648, during the 'Second Civil War'. King Charles was still a prisoner.

The King must die

Cromwell and the army officers had had enough. Some army officers began calling Charles 'a man of blood'. Charles had shown he could not be trusted. There was only one solution: the King must die. But he had to die legally after a trial, and most MPs would not allow such a trial. So in December 1648 Colonel Pride and a troop of soldiers marched into the Commons, expelled 96 MPs and arrested 41 others. The 'Rump Parliament' of MPs who were left voted by 26 votes to 20 to put the King on trial. The Lords were not consulted.

On 20 January 1649 a special court, set up by Parliament, met in Westminster Hall. Parliament chose 135 judges to try the King, but only about 85 dared to turn up. John Bradshaw, the President of the Court, wore a steel-lined hat in case a Royalist shot at him. Charles was accused of trying to destroy the liberties of his people and of causing all the misery and bloodshed in the Civil War. He refused to defend himself because he said the court was illegal.

Source A

Part of a speech made by Charles I on 21 January 1649.

Obedience to kings is strictly commanded in both the Old and New Testaments. The king can do no wrong. The law upon which you base your proceedings must be either an old law or a new one. If it is an old law, explain where it is written. If it is a new law, explain who had the authority to make it. I speak for the true liberty of all my subjects, which consists not in the power of government, but in living under such laws. The arms I took up were only to defend the fundamental laws of this kingdom.

Source B

Part of the sentence on Charles I, read out by John Bradshaw on 27 January 1649.

Charles Stuart, King of England, trusted to rule according to the laws of this land, had a wicked plan to create for himself an unlimited and unjust power to rule as he wanted. Like a traitor he waged war against Parliament and the people. He is a tyrant, traitor, murderer and enemy of the people of England.

Source C

Part of a picture of the execution of Charles I in 1649.

Many people, including Thomas Fairfax, agreed with him. The court was certain to give the verdict the army wanted. After a week, John Bradshaw sentenced his king, Charles I, to death.

The execution

On Tuesday, 30 January 1649, King Charles I stepped out of his palace at Whitehall onto the scaffold. He wore two shirts because it was a cold day and he did not want to shiver – this might have made the vast crowd think he was afraid. The executioners wore masks, with false hair and beards. Charles made a speech claiming that he had defended the law and Church of England. Then he knelt and put his head on the block. At four minutes past two it was all over: the King was dead.

Henrietta Maria

Princess Henrietta Maria of France was married to Charles I in 1625, when she was 15, and Charles was 24 years of age. The Royal court was a familiar place for Henrietta, who had spent all her life surrounded by royalty. Born in 1610, she was the youngest daughter of Henri IV of France and his queen, Marie de Médicis.

Henrietta was an unpopular match for the Protestant Charles, as she was a Catholic, but by the 1630s their marriage was being celebrated in art and literature. Henrietta herself was very fond of the arts, and enjoyed participating in court masques with her husband, the King. The famous painter, Van Dyck, made many beautiful portraits of Henrietta.

King Charles and Henrietta Maria had eight children: Charles, Mary, James, Elizabeth, Anne, Catherine, Henry and Henrietta. Out of these eight, both Charles and James were later to become kings of England. During the Civil War, Henrietta Maria went abroad to seek support for her husband. It is said that she secretly took with her the Crown Jewels, which she was prepared to pawn in return for money to help the Royalist cause. She returned to England in 1662, a widow, and lived for a short while in the Queen's House at Greenwich, which she had started to decorate before the Civil War. But England held little for Henrietta since the execution of Charles, and she returned to her native France, where she died in 1669.

5.5 OLIVER CROMWELL: PROTECTOR OR DICTATOR?

The King was dead. Parliament passed laws which abolished the monarchy, the House of Lords and the Church of England and declared England to be a Commonwealth, meaning a **republic**. But nobody really knew how the country would be governed. Who would call MPs to meet and who would say what they should do? Cromwell seemed to be the most powerful person in the country. The army and MPs expected him to take the lead.

'In the name of God, go!'

Cromwell and most of his army officers were Puritans. They believed that their victories in the Civil War proved that God was on their side. They expected Parliament to pass the sort of laws which would make England a more godly country.

But the Rump Parliament, which had agreed to the trial of Charles I, was still there and it had no intention of passing the sort of laws the army wanted. In April 1653 the MPs even suggested that they could carry on being MPs for ever, without having to be re-elected! This was too much for Cromwell. With his soldiers he went to the Commons on 20 April and expelled the MPs.

The Barebones Parliament

Cromwell and his Council of State decided that the time had come for the country to be run by 'godly men'. They selected 140 Puritans as MPs in a new parliament. This 'Barebones Parliament' was named after one of its leaders, Praise-God Barebones.

But Cromwell soon discovered that some of the new MPs had extreme views which he could not support. For example, they wanted to abolish tithes and carry out reforms to the law so that theft was no longer punishable by death. These were very extreme views for the time. Fortunately for Cromwell, some of the more conservative MPs took fright at what was happening and voted to end the Parliament.

Source A

An account of Cromwell's words to the Rump Parliament in 1653, written by Bulstrode Whitelock, who was an MP and in the Commons at the time.

'Take away that fool's bauble, the mace. You have sat too long here for any good you have been doing. Depart, I say, and let us have done with you. In the name of God, go!'

A Dutch picture from the time showing Cromwell dismissing the Rump Parliament.

Source B

Lord Protector

Cromwell now decided that he ought to play a more direct role in governing the country. He accepted a document drawn up by some of his army officers called 'The Instrument of Government' which set up a government called the Protectorate. Cromwell was made head of that government with the title 'Lord Protector', although in theory he had to share power with a newly appointed Council of State. The Instrument of Government also said that only 'god-fearing' men could become MPs.

The rule of the major-generals

The Protectorate faced opposition not only from those who wanted the King restored, but also from people who resented the growing power of the army. Cromwell was forced to take strong measures. In the summer of 1655 he divided the country into eleven districts and put an army major-general in charge of each district. These new rulers were responsible for rounding up opposition to Cromwell and for bringing about a godly way of life. Restrictions were placed on ale-houses, and horse-racing, dancing and the performing of plays were banned.

King Cromwell

Not surprisingly, the rule of the major-generals proved very unpopular and soon came to an end. Many people longed for an end to these experiments in government.

The only kind of stability they knew was that of a monarchy. But they did not want the Stuarts back. So in February 1657 Parliament offered the crown to Cromwell. He refused. He and his supporters in the army could not forget that they had fought long and hard to get rid of the monarchy.

He was also concerned that some people said that he had been working just to make himself king. So the Protectorate continued as Cromwell's health began to decline.

In August 1558 a visitor described the Protector as 'looking like a dying man'. Within weeks, on 3 September 1658 Cromwell was dead.

Source C

The Lord Protector rules the people with Parliament and the Council. Rules with the Council when Parliament not sitting. Can dismiss Parliament. Cannot make war or peace without consent of the Council of State.

The Council of State contains civilian and army members. Helps the Lord Protector rule. Selected by Parliament.

The people Men owning property valued at more than £200 can vote and pay taxes.

Women cannot vote.

This is how the country was governed under the Protectorate.

Oliver Cromwell

Born in Huntingdon in 1599, Oliver Cromwell was the son of a well-to-do landowner. He was married to Elizabeth, the daughter of a wealthy merchant. His involvement in the Civil War brought him to the forefront of politics. Cromwell had studied at Cambridge, and then pursued law in London, before his father died in 1617, leaving him the estate in Huntingdon.

Cromwell was not a handsome man, but cared little about this, ordering his artist to paint him 'warts and all'. He was remembered by many as a devoutly religious man with few illusions and little vanity, but with a strong determination and will to succeed. He died in 1658, aged 59.

A melting pot of ideas

For many people the world had been turned upside down. They had killed their king and Cromwell was trying out all kinds of new ideas about how to rule. Ordinary people began to have their own ideas, too. Some of these ideas had been around in secret for years. Now, under the Protectorate, people felt free to talk about them, write about them and sometimes put them into practice.

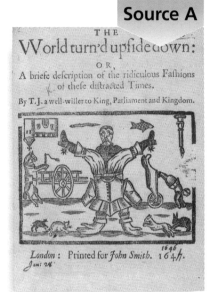

Source A

THE
World turn'd upfide down:
OR,
A briefe defcription of the ridiculous Fafhions
of thefe diftracted Times.

By T.J. a well-willer to King, Parliament and Kingdom.

London : Printed for John Smith. 1646
Jan. 26.

The front cover of a pamphlet called *The World Turned Upside Down*, published in about 1647.

Fifth Monarchists

This group believed that Christ was about to win the battle between good and evil and would rule the earth as the 'Fifth Monarch'. They had to make England a suitable place for Christ. They wanted a Parliament of godly people, not elected MPs. It was more important to be God-fearing than to be a gentleman.

Diggers

The Diggers, led by Gerrard Winstanley, believed that no one person should rule over another. All men were equal and had an equal right to a share in the land. They believed people should live without private property. They set up a community on a hill in Surrey to show how it could be done. At first there were just small groups in the south and east, but gradually Digger groups appeared all over the country.

Muggletonians

The Muggletonians were led by John Reeve and Ludowicke Muggleton. They believed in the coming of God's Kingdom on earth, and that God had given them the power to decide who should be damned and who should be saved.

NOW CHRIST'S COMING TO STAY ON THURSDAY — WHO'S GOT A SPARE ROOM?!

WE'VE GOT IT ALL WORKED OUT. STOP ARGUING AND READ THIS BOOK

THE BULL INN SHOPSGATE

WISDOM 97

Levellers

This group, led by John Lilburne, said that true power lay with the people, although they could give some of it up to Parliament. This meant more people should be able to vote. They wanted to lessen the power of Parliament, reduce taxes and help tenant farmers against landlords. They had a lot of support, particularly in hard times.

"I UNDERSTAND YOU GOD, WHAT DO YOU WANT ME TO DO NOW?

QUAKERS SAY LISTEN TO GOD AND DON'T PAY TITHES AND DON'T SWEAR ON THE BIBLE

"I CAN DO NO WRONG! GOD SAID SO!

Quakers

These were people who listened to the voice of the Holy Spirit within them, rather than the teachings of the Church. They believed all people were equal. They refused to pay tithes to the official Church, and would not swear on the Bible in a law court. By 1700 there were about 40,000 Quakers in Britain.

Ranters

These were a small group of people who believed they had been specially chosen by God and could do no wrong. They did not believe in the teachings of the Bible or the Anglican Church, but obeyed the Holy Spirit inside themselves.

"LISTEN TO THEM! TAKE IT FROM ME, WELL HAVE A KING AGAIN AT THIS RATE!

What a weirdo.

Gerrard Winstanley

The leader of the Diggers, Gerrard Winstanley was born in 1609. He worked until the 1640s as a cloth merchant in London. When his business failed, Winstanley devoted his life to the Diggers. He believed that God gave the earth to all His creatures, not just those with enough money to buy land. He died in 1676.

One of the groups that existed under the Protectorate was the 'Levellers'. This group was made up from soldiers in the New Model Army who wanted Parliament to represent everyone, not just rich landowners like Cromwell. Most Levellers were ordinary craftsmen and farmers, who thought that one of the reasons for fighting the Civil War was to get more representation. They felt betrayed by Cromwell, who had not brought about these changes.

Many of the soldiers in the New Model Army were angry with Cromwell anyway, because their wages had not been paid for a long time. The Levellers were especially angry because they thought that Cromwell was trying to shut them up and keep them away, by sending them to fight the rebels in Ireland.

Some of them decided that they would not let Cromwell treat them this way.

The march to Burford

In 1649 a group of Levellers found out they were to be sent to fight in Ireland. Cromwell had promised that soldiers would not be forced to go to Ireland against their wishes. So the Levellers wrote a letter of complaint to their Colonel, explaining that:

we cannot, in duty to God, this Nation, and our fellow soldiers, fight in Ireland.

The Levellers did not wait for a reply. They left their regiment and marched through Wiltshire to Oxfordshire, picking up supporters from other regiments on their way. On 13 May they reached Burford, an Oxfordshire village. They decided to rest there for the night.

Source A

This was carved into the lead font in Burford church during the three nights' imprisonment. Sedley was one of the men made to watch the execution in the churchyard.

Source B

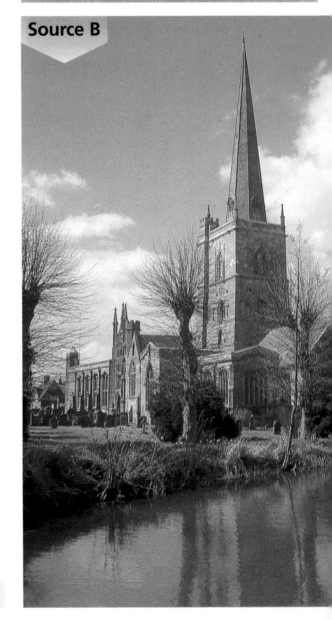

Burford church and churchyard.

Source C

A few days after the troops left Burford, the churchwardens made this entry in the account book.

To Daniel Munke and others for cleaning the church when the Levellers were taken – 3s 6d.

Cromwell attacks!

No sooner had the Levellers settled for the night than they were rudely awakened. According to a Leveller pamphlet, written at the time: *Cromwell's forces came pouring in on both sides of Burford, and violently fell upon us, plundered us, stripped us, and treated us worse than Cavaliers.*

Cromwell thought the Levellers were little better than **mutineers**, and he decided to deal with them himself. During the attack 340 Levellers were locked in the Burford church, where Cromwell told them that they were all sentenced to death. The Levellers spent three nights in the church, believing they were about to be killed. One of them carved his name into the lead of the font (see Source A).

Source D

A fourth man, Cornet Den, was also due to be executed, but when his time came he begged for forgiveness, admitting everything he had done was wrong, and Cromwell lifted his sentence. The Levellers therefore saw him as a traitor, and their pamphlet, printed immediately after the event, does not speak kindly of him.

Den preached his apology to Cromwell in the Pulpit of Burford Church, stated the unlawfulness of our actions, and justified the wicked deeds of Cromwell and his generals, howling and weeping like a crocodile. This makes him a perfect rogue and villain upon everlasting record.

An Agreement of the People

The Levellers' aims were put forward in their document called *An Agreement of the People*, in 1647:

- All men should be equal in the eyes of the law.
- Parliament should meet every two years and represent the needs of everyone – not just the rich.
- All men should be allowed to vote, except for servants and paupers.
- All religions should be tolerated.
- Tithes (the tax paid to the Church) should be abolished.
- Capital punishment should be abolished, except for murder and treason.

Execution

On the fourth day, the prisoners were told that only the ringleaders would be killed. The rest were led up the turret to the church roof, where they watched the execution of three of their fellow men in the churchyard: *Cromwell stood by to see Cornet Tomson, Master Church, and Master Perkins murdered.*

The men were shot to death under Cromwell's orders, by his loyal troops. By executing the three Levellers, Cromwell made it clear that the Levellers' ideas were too extreme for his liking, and too dangerous because of their popularity. He was also making the point that he would not tolerate extreme elements in his army.

John Lilburne

Lilburne (1614–57) was a leading supporter of the Levellers. His pamphlet 'The Foundations of Freedom', putting forward the Levellers' beliefs, was presented to Parliament in 1649. The government was very worried about Lilburne and he was frequently imprisoned. In 1663 the Leveller group was banned.

5.8 ELIZABETH DYSART: DOUBLE AGENT OR LOYAL ROYALIST?

Late in August 1658 a small boat slipped across the English Channel at the dead of night. It was on its way to France, carrying Elizabeth, Countess of Dysart. She was the wife of Sir Lionel Tollemache, a wealthy Suffolk landowner and loyal supporter of Charles I during the Civil War. Elizabeth's official reasons for going abroad were that she had property in Holland and one of her children lived in Paris. But why was she travelling so secretly? Some people believe that she was carrying secret messages to Royalists in France.

The young Royalist

Elizabeth was fifteen when the Civil War broke out in 1642. She was living with her parents, William and Catherine Murray, and her three younger sisters at Ham House in Surrey. King Charles I was a frequent visitor. Elizabeth's father and the King had been brought up together when they were boys and remained firm friends into their adult lives. So it was not surprising that when the Civil War broke out William Murray joined the King's side. He quickly became a trusted messenger, carrying letters between Charles and his Queen, Henrietta Maria, who was in exile in Holland. Charles was grateful, and made him Earl of Dysart. William carried on working as the King's secret agent. He tried, and failed, to negotiate an agreement between Charles and the Scots. After Charles' execution, William spent most of the rest of his life in exile in Holland. Maybe it was during this time that Elizabeth learned about the dangerous – and exciting – life of a secret agent.

Cromwell's friend

After the execution of Charles, Elizabeth Dysart began playing a very dangerous game. She and her husband divided their time between Ham House and their estates in Suffolk. There were some surprising guests at their homes. Oliver Cromwell was a welcome visitor at both their houses and they often went to Cromwell's court.

A portrait of Elizabeth Dysart painted when she was a young woman.

Source B

Bishop Burnet (1643–1715) describes Elizabeth Dysart in *History of his own Times*.

She had a wonderful quickness of understanding and an amazing liveliness in conversation.

She had studied not only divinity and history, but mathematics and philosophy.

She was violent in every thing she set about, a violent friend, but a still more violent enemy.

Elizabeth became a close friend of Cromwell's wife, and by 1651 there were strong rumours that Elizabeth was Cromwell's mistress. But it was more likely that the Dysarts were simply trying to keep in with both sides – a common practice in these troubled times.

The 'Sealed Knot'

Elizabeth was a leading member of a secret society called the 'Sealed Knot'. The society's aim was to put Charles I's son, Charles Stuart, on the throne of England. They passed messages between Charles, who was in exile in Europe, and his supporters in England. Safe houses were set up where letters were left addressed to 'Mr Sloane', 'Mrs Grey' or 'Mr Lawton'. These letters found their way to Charles. A London pub called 'The Sign of the Rose' collected letters from France, which were written in code, often using invisible ink. They were then passed on to Elizabeth Dysart. After Oliver Cromwell's death the Secret Service intercepted all Elizabeth's letters and most of them ended up in the hands of government officials.

A double agent?

A double agent is someone who works for both sides at the same time. Was Elizabeth a double agent, working for both Cromwell and Charles Stuart? She seems to have tried to work out a compromise between them. The idea was that Charles would return to England as king and Cromwell would be his Chief Minister. Cromwell's wife was very much in favour of this, but Cromwell himself was not a stupid man and was suspicious of where an arrangement like that would lead!

And finally ...?

When Charles Stuart was restored to the throne of England in 1660 he gave Elizabeth a pension of £800 as a reward for all she had done for the Royalist cause. In 1672 Elizabeth, now a widow, married the Earl of Lauderdale, a very powerful man in Charles II's government.

Source C

In the autumn of 1656, Sir Richard Browne, Charles Stuart's chief official in Paris, was keeping a close watch on Elizabeth Dysart. He believed she could be a double agent because he could not find out what she was up to. He reported:

The lady Tollemache, Mr William Murray's daughter, is come to Paris. When I can learn anything more particularly of her, and where she is, I will tell your Honour. What she intends I have not learnt.

Source D

The Royalist, Sir John Reresby wrote this in his memoirs on 13 May 1677.

The next day I went to visit the Duke and Duchess of Lauderdale at their fine house at Ham. After dinner, her Grace entertained me in her chamber with much discourse upon affairs of state. She had been a beautiful woman, and was the supposed mistress of Oliver Cromwell.

Bishop Gilbert Burnet

Bishop Burnet (1643–1715) was a talented scholar who was fluent in a number of languages, including Hebrew. At the age of 26 he was appointed Professor of Divinity at Glasgow University, but was not popular with Charles II who had him dismissed. Burnet travelled widely in Europe and met William of Orange, who later appointed him as Bishop of Salisbury. Burnet had three wives. It is said that one was famous for her beauty, the next for her money and the last for her piety.

No more Protectors

In 1657 Cromwell had refused to accept the throne of England. He did not want to be king and the army was opposed to the restoration of the monarchy. But this presented a problem. What would happen when Cromwell died? In many ways the situation was just like it would have been if Cromwell had been made king. His son took over!

However, Oliver's son, Richard Cromwell, who became Lord Protector in 1658, did not have the full support of the army, or of Parliament. In 1659 he resigned and a senior army officer, General Monck, brought his army to London and recalled the Long Parliament. This was the original parliament of 1640 and contained many supporters of the monarchy. Monck knew that it would almost certainly ask Charles II to return from exile in Holland to take over as king.

The Restoration

There were, of course, some important decisions to be made before Charles could return. For example, what would happen to those people who opposed Charles I in the Civil War? Would they be punished? What would be done about the land that had been taken from the King, the lords, the Royalists and the Church of England, and then sold (much of it to people who were at present in Parliament)? And of course what arrangements would be made for the Church? Would Charles allow religious toleration? Charles knew exactly what he should say to make himself popular. In the Declaration of Breda (1660) he agreed that these matters could be sorted out by discussions between King and Parliament.

The new King

Charles was greeted with great enthusiasm on his return to England in May 1660. Many people had disliked the harsh and oppressive rule of Cromwell. They wanted to see a king who was fun and who had the dignity and bearing expected of a monarch. Charles fitted this description perfectly. He loved the ceremony and pomp of monarchy and enjoyed dancing, drinking wine and visits to Newmarket to watch the horse racing. All this earned him the nickname 'The Merry Monarch'. But compared to Oliver Cromwell most people might appear 'merry'.

Source A

A portrait of Charles II painted during his reign.

Source B

Titus Oates in the pillory.

What was restored?

1 Charles told Parliament that he was prepared to show mercy to those who had opposed his father. But Parliament was less generous. It ordered Oliver Cromwell's body to be dug up and hanged, and then the head to be displayed on London Bridge. Thirteen of those people involved in the execution of Charles I were also hanged. However, most of those who fought against Charles in the Civil War were pardoned.

2 Royalists whose land had been confiscated during the Protectorate had it restored, but most of those who had sold it did not.

3 The House of Lords was restored with the bishops of the Church of England sitting in it.

4 The Church of England was restored. Various acts passed by Parliament made all other types of church service illegal and stopped anyone who was not a member of the Church of England from being an MP, town councillor, priest or teacher. So Catholics and Dissenters became almost second class citizens in Restoration England.

Source C

An account of Oates receiving his punishment, written in 1686.

I heard a friend of my father say that he saw Titus Oates, that discovered the Popish Plot, whipped most miserably. And as he was going along the street the crowd took pity on him and cried to the hangman (whose job it was to whip him) 'Enough! Strike easy! Enough!'

The Popish Plot

The importance that was still attached to religion at this time can be seen in the extraordinary events of the 'Popish Plot' of 1678. A clergyman, Titus Oates, informed the Privy Council of a plot by Catholics to kill the King. Charles does not seem to have believed the story and many councillors were also deeply suspicious of Oates' evidence. But when a magistrate called Sir Edmund Berry Godfrey was murdered they changed their minds. Godfrey had been the person to whom Oates had originally told his story. There then followed a period of anti-Catholic hysteria in which 35 innocent Catholics were accused of plotting against the King and executed. Charles' brother and heir, James Duke of York, who was a Catholic, was forced to live abroad until the hysteria died down. Finally Oates was revealed as a liar. In May 1685 he was sentenced to a massive fine, to stand in the **pillory** and to be **flogged** once a year, as well as imprisoned for life (though in 1689 he was released).

Richard Cromwell

When Oliver Cromwell died at Whitehall Palace in 1658, his son, Richard, took over as Lord Protector. Richard was born in 1626, the youngest of Oliver's three sons, but the early deaths of his brothers Robert and Oliver left him as Cromwell's heir. He was a pleasant man, who enjoyed field sports, but he lacked his father's strength and confidence.

Not long after he took up the post of Lord Protector, the campaign to restore the monarchy broke out, and Richard abdicated, deep in debt, in 1659. Richard lived abroad under the false name 'John Clarke', but later returned to England, where he died in 1712 at the great age of 86!

The Exclusion Crisis

The Popish Plot revealed a fear of the return of Catholicism in the country. This led to attempts to exclude Charles' brother, James, from the throne because he was a Catholic. However, Charles was clever enough to defeat his opponents. Therefore, when he died in 1685 (shortly after he himself had been admitted into the Catholic Church) James became king.

The new King

Despite being a Catholic James was welcomed by most English people. He had shown himself to be a brave soldier and, unlike Charles, was hardworking. So people were prepared to overlook his own religious beliefs.

In the first year of his reign there were two uprisings against him, one in Scotland led by the Duke of Argyll and one in England led by Charles' illegitimate son, the Duke of Monmouth. Both were easily defeated. In England, Monmouth's defeat resulted in severe punishments issued by Judge Jeffreys. Over 200 rebels were hanged, drawn and quartered and 800 sold to the West Indies as slaves.

Although James had been popular at the start of his reign, his attempts to promote Catholicism soon made him very unpopular. He began appointing Catholics as government ministers, and reversed laws preventing Catholics from serving in the army and local government. In 1687 he stated that his ideal aim was to have 'all his subjects as members of the Catholic Church'. In the same year he dissolved Parliament, which was made up of members of the Church of England, and so opposed his religious policies.

Another James

James was fifty-four in 1687 and would be succeeded by his elder daughter, Mary. Since she was a Protestant, people knew that James could not expect to restore the Catholic faith permanently.

In June 1688 James' second wife gave birth to a son, James. This boy would be brought up as a Catholic and could rule for many years. Some of James' opponents suggested that the Queen had not really been pregnant and that the boy had been smuggled into the royal bed in a warming pan!

Source D

Extract from a pamphlet printed in London in 1679.

Imagine a troop of Catholics ravishing your wives and daughters, dashing your little children's brains out against the walls, plundering your houses and cutting your throats. Cast your eye towards Smithfield, imagine you see your father or mother tied to the stake in the midst of the flames. With heads and eyes lifted up to heaven they scream and cry out to God, for whose cause they die. This was a frequent spectacle last time the Catholics ruled amongst us.

Source E

Robert Walpole addressing the Cabinet.

The 'Glorious Revolution'

Since they did not want another Catholic king, a group of senior Members of Parliament opposed to James' politics sent a message to Mary's husband, William. They asked him to come to England to restore the English people's 'true liberties'. William landed with an army on 5 November 1688 and marched to London. On hearing that William had landed, James fled the country. Supporters of parliamentary government now talk of this event as a 'Glorious Revolution'. The domineering and Catholic James had been replaced by William and Mary, monarchs chosen by Parliament.

Restrictions on the monarchy

It was during the reign of William and Mary that a series of laws were passed which placed restrictions on the king and confirmed the rights of Parliament. From now on there were rules about how often Parliament should meet and even who was eligible to be king. This marked the beginning of a system of government in Britain where Parliament and monarch governed the country together.

Restrictions placed on the monarchy by the end of the Stuart period.

Later developments

Mary and William had no children and so when William died in 1702 (Mary had died in 1694) Mary's sister Anne became Queen. She died in 1714, with no living children, and was succeeded by James I's great grandson, George I. He was Elector of Hanover, and so he is said to be the first of the Hanoverian kings. It was in his reign that the modern system of having a Prime Minister chairing a Cabinet developed. Sir Robert Walpole is often said to be Britain's first Prime Minister, although it was many years later before the title was widely used.

Judge Jeffreys

George Jeffreys (1648–1689) was a judge during the reigns of Charles II and James II. He was so severe on those found guilty in his courts that he earned the nickname 'the Hanging Judge'.

In 1685 James II made him a baron. In the same year Jeffreys conducted a series of trials against those suspected of involvement in Monmouth's rebellion. Most were hanged. When James II fled the country in 1688 Jeffreys was arrested and imprisoned in the Tower of London.

Gaelic princes and English lords

The English first came to Ireland in the Middle Ages when a group of Norman barons settled there. In 1500 Ireland was run by a combination of **Gaelic**-speaking Irish princes and English lords. The Irish princes kept their own armies and ran their lands according to Gaelic laws and customs. English law held good only in the lands of the English lords. It was strongest around Dublin, in an area called the Pale. There a Lord Deputy ruled on behalf of the English monarch, helped by a Council and a Parliament. Outside the Pale members of the Gaelic and English ruling families married each other, and Gaelic people often lived on land belonging to English lords.

Reformation and rebellion

During the reign of Henry VIII, English religion broke free from the control of the Pope in Rome. Henry wanted to do the same in Ireland. Some Irish leaders were happy to buy lands which had previously been owned by the monasteries, but many of them were strong Catholics who objected to what Henry was doing and rebelled against English control.

The Lord Deputies, working from Dublin, tried to force the Irish to follow England's lead. They also began a policy of plantation. They seized land from Irish rebels and sold it to English settlers. This plan had two good points as far as the English were concerned. It provided money to pay for an army to be stationed in Ireland to keep control. It also meant that there were more English people in Ireland and so English law and customs spread more rapidly.

Under Queen Elizabeth, English influence grew and by the middle of her reign the English had gained control of the south and east of Ireland and re-organised it into counties.

Then, in 1595, the Earl of Tyrone decided to set himself up as leader of Gaelic Ireland. With the Earl of Tyrconnel, several English lords from southern Ireland who had remained Catholic and 3500 Spanish troops, he fought the English Protestant invaders. Elizabeth I was furious. She sent an army of 17,000 men, commanded by the Earl of Essex, to put down the rebellion. After months of bitter fighting, the earls of Tyrone and Tyrconnel surrendered. The English had now conquered the whole of Ireland.

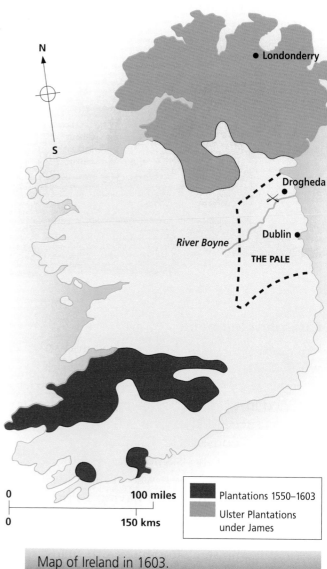

N

S

Londonderry

Drogheda

Dublin

River Boyne

THE PALE

0   100 miles

0   150 kms

Plantations 1550–1603

Ulster Plantations under James

Map of Ireland in 1603.

The Ulster Plantation

In 1607 the earls of Tyrone and Tyrconnel fled to Europe. This gave James I's advisers the chance they wanted. The government believed the Irish were dangerous and uncivilised. The only way to control the country was to send English and Scottish Protestants to live there. The English government seized the lands of the two earls. They sacked the Gaelic landlords and put Protestants in their place. These new landlords arranged for Protestants from Scotland and England to settle on their land – land that had previously been farmed by Irish Catholics.

The Irish Catholics deeply resented this Ulster **Plantation**. This resentment grew until, in 1641, they murdered several thousand of these Protestant settlers. You read (on page 54) of the problems this caused when King Charles I wanted an army to control the Catholics.

Cromwell and Drogheda

Cromwell and many Puritans believed that Charles I and his Catholic Queen, Henrietta Maria, were behind the massacre of Protestants in 1641. They feared Charles was a secret Catholic. They became even more certain when, after the execution of the King, Irish Catholics and Irish Royalists joined together in rebellion against Parliamentary rule. Parliament put Cromwell at the head of a strong army. He was going to put a stop to rebellion in Ireland once and for all.

A Parliamentarian army had defeated the rebels before Cromwell arrived. Even so, he marched up and down the east coast, besieging towns and killing Catholics. The worst of these massacres happened at Drogheda, north of Dublin, in September 1649. Cromwell and his troops laid siege to the town, which refused to surrender. When his troops finally broke through, they killed everyone they found.

Source A

An extract from a letter written by Cromwell to Parliament, September 1649.

I am persuaded that this is a righteous judgment of God upon these barbarous wretches and that it will tend to prevent the spilling of blood in the future. These are the only grounds for such action, which otherwise will bring remorse and regret.

Cromwell settles Ireland

Cromwell gave orders for hundreds of Irish rebels to be shipped off to work as slaves on the sugar estates in the Caribbean. He sent Irish landowners to Connaught, in western Ireland, and gave their land to soldiers and Protestants. Now Protestants controlled all of Ireland, even though most of the people living there were Catholic.

Source B

A picture of Irish Catholics murdering Protestant settlers. This propaganda picture made in 1641 was designed to convince English people that the Catholics were planning a wholescale massacre of Protestants in Ireland.

James II and Ireland

In the second half of the seventeenth century, the Irish were kept under careful control by their English rulers. But when the Catholic James II came to the throne in 1685, he let the Irish Catholics follow their religion without penalties and also let them send MPs to sit in the Irish Parliament. He put a Catholic general in charge of the army in Ireland.

When James fled from England in 1688, he went to France where the Catholic king, Louis XIV, helped him raise an army. Then he crossed to Ireland to join up with his Catholic supporters. He soon established himself in control and began taking land back from Protestant settlers and giving it to Catholics. Obviously the Protestants resisted what James was doing, and in 1689 the Protestant city of Londonderry shut its gates as an army led by James approached.

James was determined to take the city, but its defences were very strong. He therefore decided to starve Londonderry into submission. For sixteen weeks his forces camped outside the city, refusing to allow food supplies to the starving inhabitants.

But William III was not prepared to let James win full control of Ireland. He knew that a strong James, with French support, would be a real threat to him in England. So he sent warships laden with food to raise the siege.

Source C

This 1980s wall painting from Londonderry shows William III at the Battle of the Boyne. It was painted by a Protestant to commemorate William's victory in 1689.

Source D

An account of the siege of Londonderry by a Catholic in the city in 1689.

On 12 April the Irish army appeared at our gates. King James sent us a letter telling us to surrender. We refused.

We began sending out parties to attack the Irish army, but after a few weeks we ran out of food for the horses and had to let them go. Some were captured by the enemy. The rest died of hunger.

During May and June the enemy attacked us many times. One night they placed bombs under our walls and seven men in the room next to mine were killed. Some were in pieces.

Soon we began to run short of food. Horseflesh became a rarity and prices rose rapidly. I saw 2 shillings paid for a quarter of a small dog and 4 pence for a pint of horse blood.

Eventually we were saved by William's warships bringing food. By the end of the siege we had lost 60 men in fighting, but 15,000 men, women and children had died from hunger and disease.

The Battle of the Boyne, painted in the seventeenth century.

The Battle of the Boyne

After the siege of Londonderry, William decided that decisive action was needed. On 14 June 1690 he landed in Ireland with a force of 15,000 troops. On the bright sunny morning of 1 July, he confronted James' army at the River Boyne. William's army was larger and contained an élite unit of Dutch Blue Guards. These soldiers were among the best in Europe.

The battle raged all day, until at 5 p.m. James admitted defeat and fled from the battlefield. William's casualties had been light, but his most senior general, Schomberg, was killed. When James complained to Lady Tyrconnel that the Irish army had run away from battle, she bitterly replied: *But your Majesty won the race.* She obviously thought that James had run away faster! Shortly afterwards James fled from Ireland to safety in France.

The aftermath

After the battle, English forces quickly took control of the rest of Ireland. Although William was prepared to let Catholics practise their religion and keep their lands, Parliament had other ideas. In the following years, Catholics were treated very harshly. They were forbidden to go to Mass, attend Catholic schools, vote or hold government jobs. The Protestant English were in control. Ireland was a conquered land.

William of Orange

Born in the Netherlands, William III (1650–1702) was the son of William II of Orange, and Mary, daughter of Charles I. William was made chief magistrate in the Netherlands in 1672, to help against the French invasion. He was successful, and forced the French King Louis XIV to make peace in 1678.

In an attempt to strengthen his claim to the English throne, William married Mary, a niece of Charles II, in 1677. Mary, then aged 15, was said to have wept throughout the whole ceremony! Although William was 12 years older than Mary, he was 10 cm shorter than she was. He had a short temper and no sense of humour. William reigned jointly with Mary from 1689 until Mary died in 1694.

James VI and James I

Until 1603 England and Scotland were completely different countries. Each had its own king, own Parliament, Privy Council and Church (Kirk). But when Queen Elizabeth died without children, her cousin James VI of Scotland also became King James I of England.

From now on the two countries were to have the same monarch, but they shared very little else. As you read on page 53, the Scots were not prepared to accept the English prayer book and even invaded England to defend their Church.

Charles, King of the Scots

After the execution of Charles I, Charles' son was brought to Scotland and a group of anti-English nobles crowned him 'King of the Scots'. In September 1651 a Scottish army invaded England, but it was easily defeated by Cromwell's forces at Worcester. Charles Stuart, King of the Scots, fled into exile.

The Scots were now brought into line by Cromwell. An army of occupation stayed in Scotland to ensure law and order was maintained. The Scottish Parliament and the General Assembly of the Kirk were both closed. These measures angered the Scots who hated English soldiers on their streets and the way that important decisions about Scotland were being made in England. On the other hand, merchants became prosperous because they could trade freely with British ports at home and overseas.

A Scottish Parliament again

In 1660 Charles II became King of England and Scotland. He immediately restored the Scottish Parliament. Some Scots objected to being ruled from England, but others were prepared to accept the situation. After all, Charles II and his brother James II were Stuarts and were descended from the Scot, James VI.

Scottish resentment

When James II was chased from the throne and replaced by William III there was great resentment in Scotland and some clans in the Highlands were close to rebellion. William decided to force all the clans to swear an oath of loyalty to him by 1 January 1692. This was to have tragic consequences for the MacDonald clan.

The Massacre of Glencoe, 1692

On 29 December, Maclain MacDonald, the elderly chief of the MacDonald family, rode through a snow storm from Glencoe to Fort William to take his oath of loyalty. But the Governor told him that the oath had to be taken before the Sheriff at Inverary – 60 miles away. So MacDonald rode through the storm and reached Inverary on 2 January. But the Sheriff was away celebrating Hogmanay (New Year) and MacDonald was not able to make his oath until 6 January – almost a week after the deadline.

The delay gave William the chance to teach the Highlanders a lesson for their previous support for James II. William ordered that 120 soldiers, mostly from the Campbell clan, should be stationed in MacDonalds' houses in Glencoe. They were to say that there was no room for them at Fort William.

The Campbells were the enemies of the MacDonalds, but they were accepted because Highland custom said that feuding had to stop when hospitality was being offered.

For two weeks the Campbells lived in MacDonalds' homes until the message came that *all MacDonalds under 70 should be put to the sword*. At 5 a.m. on 13 February, the killing of men, women and children began. Some escaped the massacre only to freeze to death in the Highland snow.

The attack was a failure. Only 38 bodies were found – less than a tenth of the MacDonald clan. But the Highland Scots had seen how cruel the English could be and this merely added to the support which the exiled James II and his descendants received in later years.

An Act of Union?

The question of a complete union with England came to a head again in 1702 when Queen Anne succeeded William III. She outlived all her seventeen children. Who would rule when she was dead? Many Scots said they wanted to choose their own monarch, regardless of what the English Parliament wanted. But others saw that there was something for both sides in a closer union. The Scots would be able to trade freely with England and its colonies. With Scotland part of the United Kingdom, the government in London would never again have to worry that England's old enemy, France, would ally with Scotland.

The Act of Union was finally agreed in 1707. The Scottish Parliament voted itself out of existence by 116 votes to 83. But many Scottish MPs took large bribes to vote for union with England, so it is impossible to tell how many really wanted the Union. A new British Parliament was elected, with 513 MPs from England and Wales and 45 MPs from Scotland. Sixteen Scottish lords joined the House of Lords.

There were angry demonstrations and bloody riots on the streets of Glasgow and Edinburgh. How long would the Union last?

The Jacobites

The Act of Union was more the work of the Lowland Scots than the Highlanders. In fact, many Lowland Scots hated the Highlanders, with their strong clan system and their chiefs, more than they hated the English. Some Highlanders were still Catholic; most Lowlanders were Calvinists or Presbyterian.

The Highlanders stayed loyal to their Catholic king. Many drank toasts to the 'King over the water'. By this they meant James Edward Stuart, the son of James II, who was in exile overseas. (Look back at pages 68–71 to remind yourself of why this happened.) They longed for, and plotted for, the day when he would be their king. They were called Jacobites because *Jacobus* is the Latin for *James*.

The Jacobites thought their chance had come in 1714 when Queen Anne died, but the crown of Great Britain went to George of Hanover. The Jacobites believed James Edward Stuart had a better claim to the throne (see Source A).

Queen Anne

Queen Anne (1665–1714) was the second daughter of James II and ruled as Queen of England during 1702–14. In 1683 she married Prince George of Denmark and bore him 17 children. It is thought that only six of the babies were born alive, and only one, William, survived infancy. He died at the age of 12.
As she had no surviving children. Anne was the last of the Stuart monarchs. She was succeeded by her German cousin, George of Hanover.

The Act of Union, 1707

The Scots agreed that:

- there would be one United Kingdom Parliament. Scotland would send lords and MPs to the Parliament at Westminster
- George of Hanover would be king of the whole United Kingdom when Queen Anne died
- Scotland would use English money and English weights and measures.

The English agreed that:

- Scottish people had the same trading rights in Britain and the colonies as any English person
- Scottish people could keep their own law courts and their own Church, the Presbyterian Church.

Rebellion in 1715

The Jacobites set up their **standard** at Braemar in September 1715 and called on all people loyal to James Edward Stuart to join them. Hundreds did, but the Jacobite army was ragged and disorganised and was easily defeated by English soldiers at Sheriffmuir, near Stirling. By the time James Edward Stuart had come over from France to lead them, most Highlanders had drifted back to the hills and there was no rebellion to lead.

Rebellion in 1745

In July 1745 Bonnie Prince Charlie, James Edward Stuart's son, landed on the west coast of Scotland with a small band of followers and proclaimed his father king. Highland chieftains and their clansmen flocked to join him. They defeated a government army at the Battle of Prestonpans (outside Edinburgh) and soon controlled most of Scotland.

Charles then had to make a difficult choice. He could either stay in Scotland and build up his power there, or push on into England. His advisers said he should stay in Scotland. Charles disagreed. He thought English Catholics would hurry to join him, bringing money and soldiers with them. He was wrong. On his march through Carlisle and Preston to Derby, only 300 men joined his army of 5000, none of them important or wealthy Catholics.

At Derby Charles stopped. He was just 138 miles from London. Should he turn back, or push on to London? His advisers said, 'Turn back to Scotland.' This time Charles took their advice. Maybe he was wrong to do so. What he did not know was that the King, George II, had packed his bags and was ready to leave London.

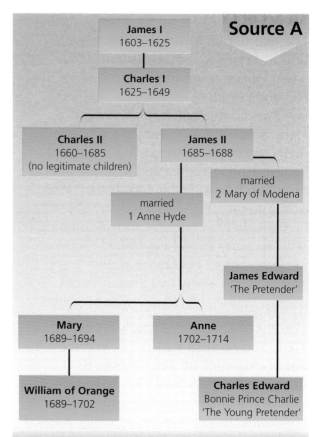

The family tree of the Stuarts. The dates given are the dates they reigned.

Bonnie Prince Charlie, 'The Young Pretender', who was born in 1720. This picture was painted during his lifetime.

Source C

This picture of the Battle of Culloden was painted by David Morier in 1746. He was paid £200 a year to work for the Duke of Cumberland.

The Battle of Culloden, 1746

When news that the Jacobites had turned back reached London, the Duke of Cumberland, King George II's son, gathered an army together and set off in pursuit. He caught them at Culloden Moor, a few miles from Inverness, and massacred them. The Jacobites who managed to escape were chased and killed without mercy. Charles escaped to France. At the end of the battle, 1200 Jacobites and 76 English soldiers were dead. The Duke of Cumberland was nicknamed 'Butcher' Cumberland because of his cruelty. The Jacobite Rebellion was over.

Gains and losses

After the 1715 rebellion, the English government built a series of forts in the Highlands. Soldiers were kept there to control the Highlanders. After the 1745 rebellion the government did its best to smash the clan system. It passed laws which destroyed the power of the clan chiefs and forced clansmen to give up their weapons and their kilts. The clan system became nothing more than a romantic memory.

On the other hand, there were gains for Scotland. By the end of the eighteenth century there were successful cotton and linen industries in the Lowlands. Glasgow was a prosperous port and Edinburgh was a centre of trade and learning. Many Scots became famous engineers, doctors, teachers and inventors, working in Britain and throughout the world.

Bonnie Prince Charlie

Prince Charles Edward Stuart was born in Italy in 1720. As a young man he was handsome, athletic, musical and skilled in many languages, including Italian, German and Spanish.

The son of James Edward Stuart, Charles was the grandson of James II, the last Catholic Stuart King of England.
After Culloden, legend has it that Bonnie Prince Charlie escaped to Skye with the help of Flora Macdonald, a local woman. She disguised him as a sewing maid, and when she objected to Charles hiding a pistol under his skirts, he joked 'If they search that far up, they'll know I'm no spinning maid!' He died in 1788.

Elves, dwarfs and imps, fairies and giants were all very real to children in Tudor and Stuart times. Their parents taught them to fear these creatures, who, they believed could turn milk sour, make a horse go lame and, worst of all, bewitch people. Adults, too, believed that spirits such as *Robin Goodfellow* and *Tom Thumb* were waiting close by, just out of sight, to do something mischievous. Thousands of men, women and children believed in these wicked spirits every bit as much as they believed in God and Jesus Christ.

Source A

This sixteenth-century woodcut shows witches standir inside a magic circle. They are swearing loyalty to the Devil. It is called *The Devil welcomes a new recruit.*

What was a witch?

Witches, it was believed, were people, mostly women, who did the Devil's work. Their power came partly from evil spirits and partly from the Devil. Witches could cause storms to happen and boats to sink; they could make a cow die and turn a child blind. Witches were easy to spot. Firstly, the Devil left a mark on their bodies, and secondly every witch had a 'familiar' – usually a cat – which could turn into a devil and do the witch's wicked work. Every old woman living alone with a cat for company was suspected!

Hunt the witch!

If a woman was suspected of witchcraft and did not confess, she was tied hand and foot and thrown into a pond or river. If she floated, she was guilty; if she sank to the bottom, she was innocent. Then in 1563 Parliament passed an act making witchcraft illegal. At least now accused people were treated more fairly, by being put on trial in front of a judge. The strange thing is that most of the accused confessed to being witches!

By the 1640s witch hunting had reached its peak. People became 'official' witch-hunters. Matthew Hopkins found 36 witches around Ipswich, in Suffolk. They were caught and tried. Thirty-four were found guilty and eighteen were hanged. Matthew called himself the 'Witch-finder General'.

By the 1750s witch hunting and fear of witches had almost died out. The last person to be persecuted for being a witch was probably old Mother Osborne, who met a terrible end in 1751 (see Source C).

Source B

John Gaule, a vicar in Huntingdonshire, did not want Matthew Hopkins anywhere near his parish. Here, in a pamphlet written in 1646, he explains why.

Every old woman with a wrinkled face, a furr'd brow, a hairy lip, a gobber tooth and a squint eye, a squeaking voice or a scolding tongue, will be called a witch.

Did you know?

Many people thought that Anne Boleyn, Henry VIII's second wife, was a witch. This was because she had three nipples, and an extra finger on one hand. They said she bewitched Henry into marrying her.

Was Mother Osborne a witch?

In April 1751 a horrifying report appeared in the *Gentleman's Magazine*.

Source C

Part of the report on the case of Mother Osborne.

At Tring, in Hertfordshire, a publican said that he was bewitched by Osborne and his wife. He had the town crier shout this at several market towns. A mob started looking for the Osbornes. They broke the windows of the workhouse and threatened to burn it down. The parish officers took the old couple from the workhouse to the church for their safety. But in order to keep the peace, the parish officers handed the old couple over to the mob. The mob stripped them naked, tied their thumbs to their toes and dragged them two miles to a muddy stream. After much ducking and abuse, the old woman, choked with mud, was thrown naked on the bank where she died. The husband had terrible bruises. The mob put the dead witch (as they called her) in bed with her husband and tied them together.

Source D

Two months later, a letter to the same magazine provided some more information.

In 1745 the old woman Osborne had come to a farmer, Mr Butterfield, and begged for some milk. But Butterfield told her, with great brutality, that he didn't have enough even for his pigs. This provoked the old woman. She told him that the Devil would have him and his pigs as well. Soon afterwards some of his calves fell ill with the distemper. Ignorant people said he had been bewitched by Mother Osborne.

One of the mob, Thomas Colley, was arrested for the murder of Ruth Osborne. He was tried at Hertford assizes and found guilty. He was executed and hanged in chains.

The ducking of Mother Osborne and her husband. This is an eighteenth-century woodcut.

Source F

This is part of what Colley wrote before he died.

It was foolish and vain imagination, heightened by strong beer, which prompted me (with others as brain mad as myself) to murder Ruth Osborne. I now declare that I do not believe there is such a thing in being as a witch.

Matthew Hopkins

Hopkins was an Essex man who appointed himself 'Witchfinder-General' and toured the local area discovering witches and having them put to death.

We know almost nothing about his early life, and it is not until 1644 that we first hear of his involvement in Manningtree in Essex, where 'there was a supposed epidemic of witchcraft'. Hopkins' ruthless interrogation of supposed witches brought about confessions and the burning of hundreds of innocent women. He disappeared from history in 1647 and some people believe that he himself was hanged for witchcraft!

Imagine waking up tomorrow and not feeling well. What would you do? Stay in bed? Watch television for the rest of the day? If you still felt unwell, perhaps you might see the doctor. No doubt you would soon be well again and return to school.

In the year 1665 thousands of people woke up not feeling well. They were not quite so calm about their illness. They had good reason to be afraid. In 1665 there was an epidemic of the dreaded plague. Plague was nothing new and most years there were people who died from it. But the 1665 outbreak was the worst for hundreds of years. It killed an estimated 110,000 people in London alone. Imagine waking up tomorrow and feeling unwell when you know that all around you people are dying of the plague! That's a different matter, isn't it?

How much of this did people know in 1665?

Since they had no idea of the existence of germs, the people at the time did not know what caused the plague. But they put forward some very original ideas such as: dry and warm weather, poisonous gases coming out of the ground, too many dogs, comets in the sky and the wrath of God. Some people took the opportunity to blame it on people they hated, such as Jews and Catholics.

Since they did not know what caused the disease, the people at the time had very little idea of how to avoid it.

What was 'the plague'?

There were three types of plague:

1 **Bubonic plague**
   This was the most common type of plague. It was caused by germs which were spread by fleas living on black rats. These fleas fed on the rat's blood by biting the rat and injecting a liquid into the blood to make it thin enough for the flea to drink. This meant the rat caught the plague and died. Then the flea jumped off the cold rat and on to the nearest warm living thing – probably a human, who then caught bubonic plague.

   Symptoms: Large swellings (called buboes) the size of chicken eggs in the armpits and groin, or smaller red spots often arranged in a circle. Temperature rising to 40.5 degrees Celsius.

   Death rate: Between 30% and 75% of people with bubonic plague died, usually after about 4 days.

2 **Pneumonic plague**
   This was also caused by germs which were spread by droplets on people's breath.

   Symptoms: The victim's saliva became slimy and tinted with blood. Then it turned bright red. Violent coughing up of blood.

   Death rate: 95% of those with this type of plague died, usually within 2 to 3 days.

3 **Septicaemic plague**
   This was when the disease spread to the blood.

   Symptoms: A sudden high fever and the face turned blue. The victim quickly fell into a coma.

   Death rate: You'd had it! Almost 100% fatality, usually on the same day.

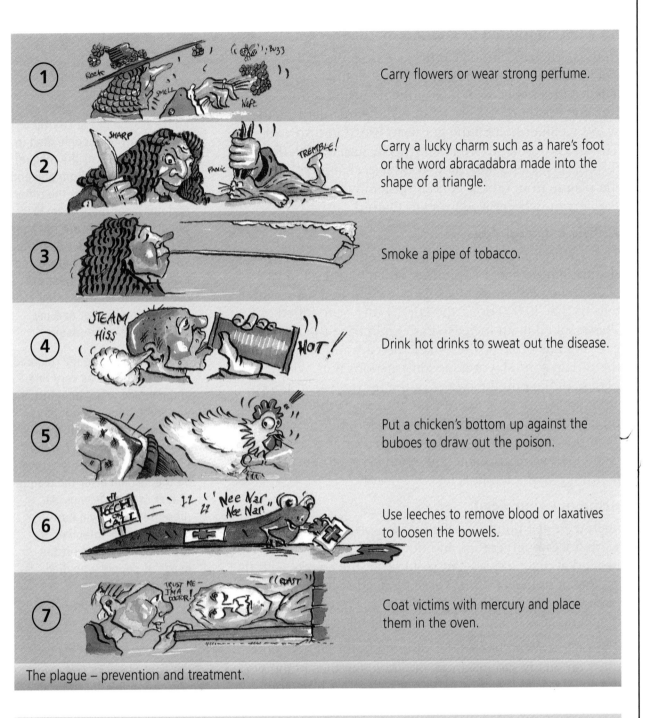

1	Carry flowers or wear strong perfume.
2	Carry a lucky charm such as a hare's foot or the word abracadabra made into the shape of a triangle.
3	Smoke a pipe of tobacco.
4	Drink hot drinks to sweat out the disease.
5	Put a chicken's bottom up against the buboes to draw out the poison.
6	Use leeches to remove blood or laxatives to loosen the bowels.
7	Coat victims with mercury and place them in the oven.

The plague – prevention and treatment.

A fate worse than death?

Because no real cure for the plague was known, the treatments could often result in severe pain, and even early death, as the pictures above show. In *A Journal of the Plague Year*, Daniel Defoe writes about how plague doctors tried to treat the swellings caused by the plague (buboes):

'The pain of the swelling was in particular very violent, and to some intolerable; the physicians and surgeons may be said to have tortured many poor creatures even to death. They applied violent drawing plasters to break the buboes, and if these did not work they cut them open and lanced them in a terrible manner.'

So what happened in London in 1665?

In the early part of the year there were few deaths, but from early June the numbers rose dramatically. The poorest areas, with their unhygienic and crowded housing conditions, were hardest hit, particularly as the warm weather helped the germs to breed and spread. Those who could afford it left the city and travelled to the countryside, where they stood less chance of catching the plague from others. Amongst them were the King and Parliament, who moved away to Oxford.

Killing cats and dogs

Those who remained had to live with the effects of the plague. Since some people believed that dogs and cats caused the plague, many of them were killed. One writer tells us that 40,000 dogs and 20,000 cats were killed. This resulted in an increase in the number of plague-carrying rats because there were no cats and dogs to kill them! The Lord Mayor issued instructions that, where plague broke out, the owner of the house was to inform an Examiner straight away. The house was then boarded up, a red cross was painted on the door and the words *Lord have mercy upon us* were written on it. Two watchmen were appointed for each house to ensure that none of the family left.

Bring out your dead!

Such were the numbers killed by the plague that there were not enough coffins and not enough individual graves. Instead at night a dead-cart would tour the streets with the cry *Bring out your dead!* Then the dead were taken to large plague-pits and tipped in. Their bodies were covered in quicklime and then the pit was hastily filled in.

The plague brought terrible suffering to the people and there are many sad instances of whole families being wiped out in a boarded-up house. Pepys tells us of how some parents smuggled their children out of plague-ridden houses in the hope that they would survive. But Daniel Defoe mentions parents who ran away from their infected children and left them to die. He also heard a story of plague victims in Portsmouth throwing the plasters from their sores into the windows of non-plague houses in the middle of the night.

Source A

Samuel Pepys writing in September 1665.

I have stayed in the city till more than 7400 people died in one week (6102 of the plague), until I could walk from one end of Lombard Street to the other and not meet more than 20 people. The nights are too short to conceal the burials of those who died the night before and I cannot find either meat or drink safe to consume. My butcher, my brewer and my baker all have the plague.

I got up and put on my coloured silk suit, which was very fine, and my new wig. I bought the wig some time ago but have not worn it because there was plague in Westminster when I bought it. I wonder what will be the fashion after the plague is over as regards wigs. At present nobody will buy any hair for fear of infection in case it has been cut off the heads of people who died of plague.

The Lord Mayor

The Lord Mayor of London was responsible for trying to stop the spread of the plague. He and his officials issued many orders, but they had no real idea what caused the plague – or how to stop it!

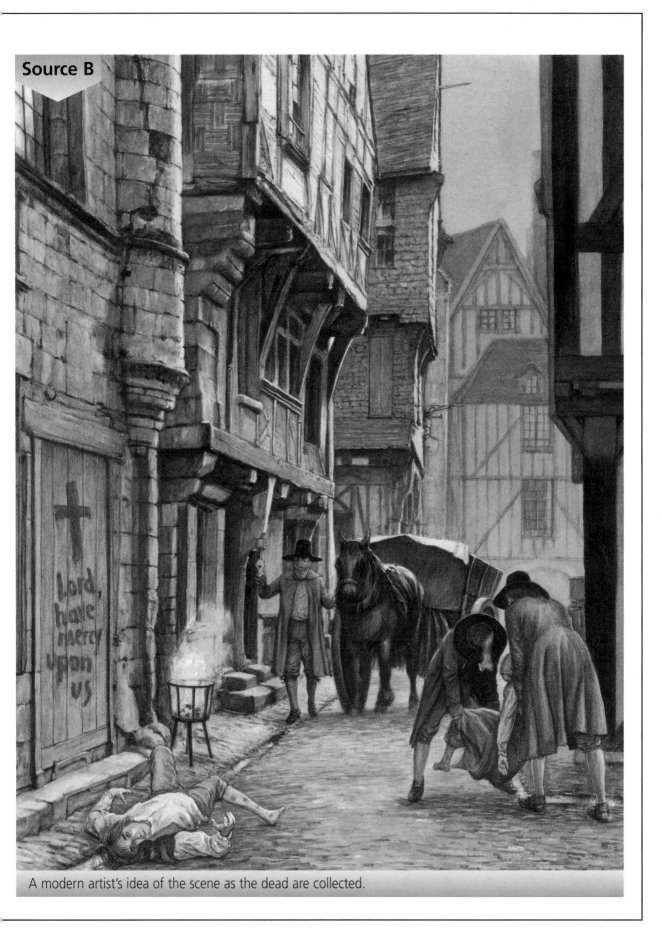

Lord, have mercy upon us

A modern artist's idea of the scene as the dead are collected.

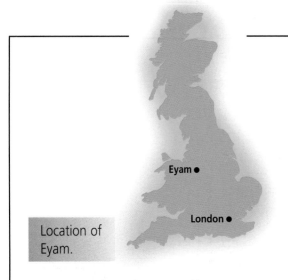

Location of Eyam.

Eyam – 'The Plague Village'

Of course the plague was not restricted just to London and there were outbreaks as far apart as Southampton and Newcastle. Many of the towns worst hit were ports or places on trade routes. One sad victim of the plague was the village of Eyam in Derbyshire.

Late in 1665 the local tailor, George Vicars, received a parcel of cloth from London. Two days later George fell ill and a few days after that he died. Then other people began feeling ill and people knew that the plague had arrived in the village. Some people began to leave, but the local vicar, William Mompesson, persuaded the villagers that if they left they might spread the disease to the rest of the county. So they decided to stay, even though they knew that they would probably catch the plague and die.

No one left the village and food was left on the outskirts. Soon people began to die and the villagers were so afraid that they refused to go to church in case they caught the disease from others. So Mompesson held his services in the open air.

Two lovers, Emmott Sydall from Eyam and Rowland Torre from nearby Stoney Middleton, were separated by the quarantine that the villagers imposed. They used to shout messages to each other across a rocky crag. One day Emmott failed to turn up. When the plague was over, Rowland found out why. Emmott was dead.

By the time the plague in Eyam had finished, 267 of the 350 inhabitants had died. One of the last victims was Catherine Mompesson, the vicar's wife. Eyam had been almost wiped out, but the plague had not spread to the rest of Derbyshire.

So how did it all end?

When autumn came in 1665 the temperature dropped and so did the number of deaths. They rose again in 1666 but fewer than 2000 deaths occurred in London. In the same year the Fire of London ravaged a great part of the town and may well have destroyed the rats, the fleas and the germs that caused the plague. The Great Plague was over.

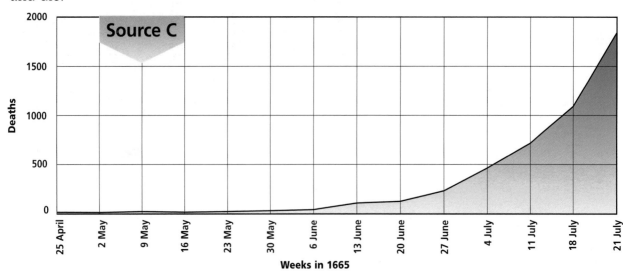

Source C

SAMUEL PEPYS

Much of our knowledge about the plague comes from the diaries of Samuel Pepys. Pepys began writing his diary in 1660 and had plenty of interesting things to comment on. In that year he travelled to Holland to escort Charles II back to England from exile. Charles gave him an important job in the Admiralty (in charge of the navy) and within a few years Pepys had witnessed the Great Plague and the Great Fire of London. He continued to write his diaries until 1669, though his career working for the government lasted until 1688. When he died in 1703 his diaries were left to Magdalene College, Cambridge. The only problem was that he had written the diaries in short hand and no one could read them! It was not until 1822 that they were decoded and a colourful picture of life in mid-seventeenth-century London emerged.

A plague doctor

When the plague broke out in 1665, doctors were as scared as anyone else about catching it, so they left the cities in great numbers, leaving very few people to try to cure the plague victims. Those doctors who did remain used all their knowledge to try to protect themselves from catching the plague.

They devised a special outfit which completely covered the body, leaving no part open to the infected air. A long leather gown was worn with leather breeches, along with a leather hat and gloves. (This must have made any delicate surgery difficult!)

A leather face mask like a hood was worn under the hat. This had one, or sometimes two, glass spy-holes in it, so that the doctor could see where he was going. A breathing-mask, shaped like a beak, was fitted into the hood. This 'beak' was stuffed with strong-smelling herbs, to 'purify' the air that was breathed in.

To complete his protection, the plague doctor carried a big stick, to make sure infected people kept away from him.

Source A

This picture of the Fire of London was painted by someone who saw it happen.

London's burning!

On Sunday, 2 September 1666 a fire started in the house of a baker, Thomas Farrinor, who lived in Pudding Lane. Thomas and his family escaped, but a maid, who refused to jump from an upstairs window, burned to death. At first the fire did not seem serious. But there was a steady east wind blowing and the fire spread swiftly through the narrow alleys with their overhanging houses to the heart of the city. The fire raged for three days. Then the wind veered south and drove the flames back on themselves. This slowed the fire down, but did not stop it.

Who was in charge?

The Lord Mayor began ordering people to pull down houses to make **fire breaks**. They would not obey him because there was an old London law which said that anyone who destroyed a house had to pay for it to be rebuilt. Then the King and the Duke of York took control. They ordered sailors to blow up houses and so create huge fire breaks across which the flames could not leap. They posted soldiers in a circle around the part of London which was burning and ordered them to make sure the fire did not spread. Gradually the fire died down, leaving a charred and desolate city centre.

Source B

These are extracts from Samuel Pepys' diary. He lived in London during the Fire.

I saw the fire rage every way, and nobody trying to quench it [put it out]. Instead they were more concerned with saving their possessions.

The streets full of nothing but people and horses and carts loaded with goods, ready to run over one another. The churches and houses were all on fire and flaming at once, and the flames made a horrible noise.

My Lady Batten sent me a cart to carry away all my money and plate and best things. In the evening Sir W. Penn and I dug a pit in the garden and put our wine in it and my parmesan cheese as well.

I saw a poor cat with the hair all burned off the body but still alive.

Who was to blame?

The Great Fire of London was so terrible that people had to blame someone. They believed it could not have started by accident. The obvious people to blame were foreigners or Catholics.

Source E

Source C

An extract from Samuel Pepys' diary for 5 November 1666.

Sir Thomas Crew says, from what he heard at the Committee for investigating the burning of the City, that it was certainly done by a plot, it being proved by many witnesses that attempts were made in several places to increase the fire. Both in the City and the country several Papists [Catholics] had boasted that we should find the hottest weather that ever was in England.

Source D

An account by Robert Latham, a modern historian.

Robert Hubert, a London watchmaker who was born in France, was tried in October 1666 and executed. The only evidence against him was his confession, which he later denied. It does not appear to be true that he was a Catholic, as he claimed. He was, in fact, mentally ill and landed in London two days after the fire started.

This column, called the Monument, was built in 1669 near the spot where the Fire started. An inscription at the bottom says that 89 churches, 13,200 houses and 400 streets were destroyed, and that the Fire was started by Catholics. Sir Christopher Wren designed the Monument and most of the other important buildings that were built after the Fire.

Source F

David Ogg, a twentieth-century historian, explains why the fire was so severe.

The fire broke out in a street where there were stores of things likely to burn, such as pitch, tar and rope. A wind from the east blew the fire toward the centre of the city. The water pump at the north end of London Bridge was out of order. The season was dry and the wells were at their lowest.

Sir Christopher Wren

Christopher Wren (1632–1723) is one of England's most famous architects, but he was also famous in other areas. He was born in East Knowle in Wiltshire and showed his remarkable talent at an early age. By the time he was 14 he had already invented a number of scientific devices.

He became Professor of Astronomy at Oxford University in 1661. At the age of 29 he began a career in architecture and designed famous buildings such as the Sheldonian theatre in Oxford. After the Great Fire of London he rebuilt St Paul's Cathedral, his most famous work – though there are many others to chose from!

In 1603, when James I came to the throne, England did not possess any lands outside the British Isles. By 1750 Britain held lands in North America, the West Indies and India. How did this happen?

Trading companies

Most colonies began as **outposts** of trading companies. Merchants in London and other major ports such as Bristol joined forces to form these trading companies. They shared the risk of ships being lost, of goods rotting on the journey home and of hostile natives burning their ships and killing the crews. They also shared the profits.

The Hudson Bay Company began trading furs in North America in 1670. The East India Company traded in spices, saltpetre, tea and dyes; by 1647 it had 47 trading posts in India.

Settlers

Some people made deliberate decisions to leave all that they knew and settle in the new colonies. On pages 48–9 you read about the Pilgrim Fathers. They were not alone. Some people went to escape religious persecution, others to start a new and better life. The Pilgrim Fathers set up Massachusetts; Catholics could live in Maryland which was set up in 1632, and the Quakers established Pennsylvania in 1681.

Prosperity

Cotton and rum, tobacco, coffee and above all sugar poured into Britain from the new colonies, especially the West Indies. The ports that did best were those on the west coast – Bristol, Liverpool and Glasgow – as well as London. London became the centre of this new trade. Banking, insurance and trading companies flourished. The port of London was one of the busiest ports in the world. A non-stop stream of ships unloaded goods from all round the world. Some of the goods, especially sugar, were shipped out again straight away. Other goods, such as woollen cloth, ribbons and tin pans, were brought by canal and wagon from within Britain to be exported.

How colonies were gained

1655	Cromwell captures **Jamaica**.
1660	Charles II is given **Bombay** as a wedding present.
1664	New Amsterdam (**New York**) is captured from the Dutch.
1704	**Gibraltar** is captured from Spain.
1688–1713	Wars with France. Britain gains **Newfoundland**, **Nova Scotia** and **Hudson's Bay**.

Source A

William Bradford, one of the leaders of the Puritan settlers in America, wrote in 1645 about what it had been like in 1620.

They had no friends to welcome them, no houses. What could they see but a desolate wilderness, full of wild beasts and wild men? If they looked behind them there was the mighty ocean as a gulf to separate them from all the civilised parts of the world.

Source B

This picture of Broad Quay, Bristol, was painted in 1720. Bristol became the second largest English city after London. Much of its wealth came from the slave trade.

Source C

A cargo ship being built in the East India Company's dockyard on the River Thames.

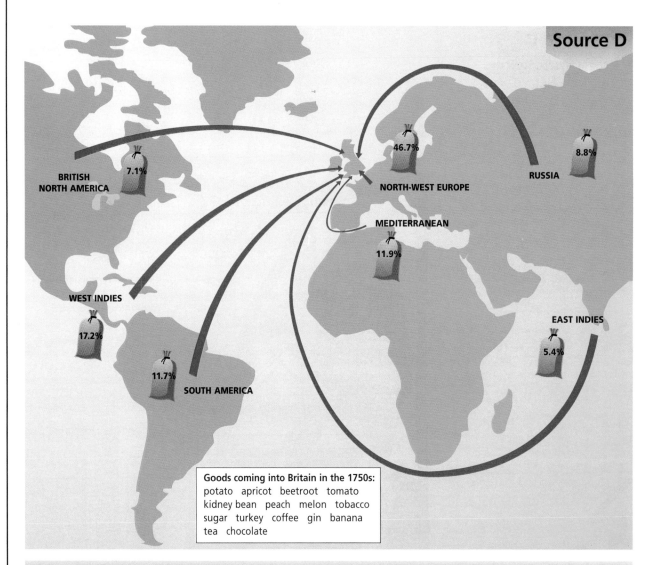

Source D

BRITISH
NORTH AMERICA 7.1%

NORTH-WEST EUROPE 46.7%

RUSSIA 8.8%

MEDITERRANEAN 11.9%

WEST INDIES 17.2%

SOUTH AMERICA 11.7%

EAST INDIES 5.4%

Goods coming into Britain in the 1750s:
potato apricot beetroot tomato
kidney bean peach melon tobacco
sugar turkey coffee gin banana
tea chocolate

This map shows the goods that were coming into Britain in the 1750s, and the parts of the world from which they came. The percentages show how much of Britain's foreign goods was coming from each region.

Sugar and slaves

Some merchants realised that enormous profits could be made from the slave trade. Ships sailed from London, Liverpool, Glasgow and Bristol laden with cloth, pots and pans, and guns. Merchants used these to trade for black slaves from African tribesmen. They then sailed to the West Indies, where they traded these slaves for rum, tobacco, sugar and raw cotton.

The most profitable thing to trade was sugar. Sugar was needed in Britain to sweeten tea, coffee and chocolate and to make puddings, creams, trifles and cakes. British merchants

shipped hundreds of tonnes of sugar to European countries and made profits from this, too. Sugar was grown in plantations worked by slaves. So hundreds of merchants made money from slavery directly or indirectly because they traded in sugar.

British merchants made huge profits. They either spent these on land and houses, or invested in industry and business. Sometimes they did both! More and more ships were built, and small ports became great trading centres.

Source E

A picture of a London coffee house, painted in 1705. By 1750 there were around 600 coffee houses in London. Here merchants, politicians and businessmen met to do deals, set up companies, plot against their political and business rivals, scheme, exchange news, swap information from the colonies and gossip. They read the daily papers and, of course, drank coffee.

Source F

This advertisement appeared in the *London Daily Journal* on 28 September 1728. (From about 1702 Fleet Street, in London, became the centre of a new industry, newspaper publishing.)

To be sold, a negro boy, aged eleven years. Enquire of the Virginia Coffee House in Threadneedle Street, behind the Royal Exchange.

Source G

This description was written by Daniel Defoe in his *Tour Through the Whole Island of Great Britain*, which was published in the 1720s.

Bristol merchants have a very great trade abroad. No cargo is too big for them. The shopkeepers in Bristol have a great inland trade. They employ carriers to all the main towns.

Coffee history

Until the seventeenth century, the only hot drinks popular in England were warm milk and mulled ale. Coffee, tea and hot chocolate were all introduced in the Stuart period. Of the three, coffee was the most popular, introduced from Arabia in about 1650.

It is believed that coffee was first brought to London in 1652 by Mr Edwards, a merchant from Turkey, who brought home with him a Greek servant called Pasqua.

This servant knew how to roast and serve coffee, and so he set up a coffee house in Lombard Street in London. Soon there were coffee shops to be found in all the large cities.

As you can read above, these houses became important meeting places for business men, and huge financial institutions such as the Stock Exchange and Lloyds of London grew from these coffee-house meetings.

Source A

This picture of the coronation of King Charles II was painted at the time.

Daniel Defoe was a reporter and a spy, a merchant and a story-teller. He was a Protestant who fought against his king. He was a businessman who went bankrupt and a political writer who was thrown into prison. He told things as he saw them, and what he didn't see, he made up.

Beginnings

Daniel Defoe was born in London in 1660 when many people were celebrating the restoration of the Stuarts and the coronation of King Charles II. The young Daniel was sent to a Presbyterian school and then to a famous academy for Dissenters. Clearly his father wanted him to become a Presbyterian minister. Daniel, however, had other ideas. Around 1684 Daniel seems to have used his wife Mary's dowry to set up as a stocking merchant. At first his business was successful and he travelled a lot in Europe. However, in 1692 it went bankrupt. Daniel managed to salvage enough money to buy a brick and tile factory. But eleven years later that, too, went bankrupt.

Defoe the spy

Daniel Defoe hated Catholicism. In 1685 he joined the Duke of Monmouth's rebellion against King James II. It was unsuccessful (see page 70) and Daniel was lucky to escape with his life.

Daniel Defoe got a government job in 1695 and added 'De' to his surname 'Foe'. Perhaps he thought it sounded posh! But then he began doing something very dangerous. He started writing articles and pamphlets which, amongst other things, poked fun at the Anglican Church. By 1703 Defoe was in prison for writing anti-government propaganda.

Source B

A
TOUR
Thro' the whole ISLAND of
GREAT BRITAIN,
Divided into
Circuits _or_ Journies.
GIVING

A Particular and Diverting Account of Whatever is Curious and worth Observation, _Viz._

I. A Description of the Principal Cities and Towns, their Situation, Magnitude, Government, and Commerce.
II. The Customs, Manners, Speech, as also the Exercises, Diversions, and Employment of the People.
III. The Produce and Improvement of the Lands, the Trade, and Manufactures.
IV. The Sea Ports and Fortifications, the Course of Rivers, and the Inland Navigation.
V. The Publick Edifices, Seats, and Palaces of the Nobility and Gentry.

With Useful Observations upon the Whole.

Particularly fitted for the Reading of such as desire to Travel over the ISLAND.

_By a_ Gentleman.

LONDON:
Printed, and Sold by G. Strahan, in _Cornhill._
W. Mears, at the _Lamb_ without _Temple-Bar._
R. Francklin, under _Tom's_ Coffee-house, _Covent-Garden._
S. Chapman, at the _Angel_ in Pall-Mall.
R. Stagg, in _Westminster-Hall,_ and
J. Graves, in St. _James's-Street._ MDCCXXIV.

The title page of Daniel Defoe's _A Tour Through the Whole Island of Great Britain_ which was published between 1724 and 1727.

Robert Harley, the Speaker of the House of Commons, had him released on condition Defoe became a secret agent. His job was to encourage pro-government feelings amongst ordinary people.

Defoe the writer

From 1704 to 1713 Defoe published a twice-weekly journal called *The Review*. He wrote history books, books about magic, ghost stories and, in 1719, the story of a shipwrecked sailor, *Robinson Crusoe*. He went on to write novels and books of moral advice.

In 1722 Defoe wrote *A Journal of the Plague Year*, which was supposed to be by someone who lived through the plague. This was odd because Defoe was only about five years old at the time the plague hit London (see pages 82–7). So how did he know what happened? He probably asked people like his uncle, Henry Foe, who did live through the plague. The rest he just made up!

Between 1724 and 1727 Defoe published *A Tour Through the Whole Island of Great Britain*. This is a wonderful description of the journeys Defoe said he took around Britain at this time. But did he really make all these journeys himself? He did make some of them. But other 'journeys' were remembered from his time as a merchant when he travelled a lot; some he put together from notes and letters sent to him from friends who travelled around Britain. The rest he probably invented. Daniel Defoe died in 1731, having written over 200 books.

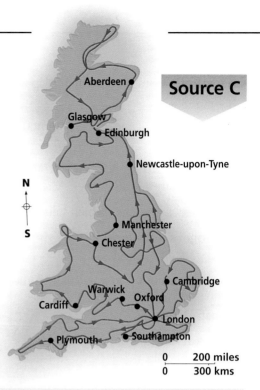

This modern map shows the journeys Defoe was supposed to have made on his 'Tour' and some of the main towns and cities he visited.

Source D

Part of Daniel Defoe's description of Warwick.

The great new church, the town-hall, the gaol, and all their public buildings are the finest in any country town in England, being all new built. The great inn at the George, the corner of the High Street, looks more like a palace. This town is counted the centre of all the horse markets and horse-fairs in England, there being no less than four fairs in a year. Here they buy horses of all sorts, for the saddle and for the coach and cart.

Robinson Crusoe

Before he wrote the novel *Robinson Crusoe*, Daniel Defoe read the true story of Alexander Selkirk, a sailor who had spent five years on a desert island near Chili. Selkirk had asked to be left there by his fellow sailors, having fallen out badly with the captain of the ship.

The story of how he survived was published in 1712, by Woodes Edward, (the captain Selkirk so hated), and in 1713 by Edward Cooke, a crew member on the ship that picked up Selkirk. Defoe was fascinated by this story and wrote *Robinson Crusoe* not long after.

GLOSSARY

anaesthetic something which stops a person feeling pain.

annulment the cancelling of something, like a marriage.

anti-clericalism opposition to the power and influence of the clergy.

antiseptic something which kills germs.

astrologers people who study the influence of the stars and planets.

clan a group of people with a common family background, especially in the Scottish Highlands.

covenant an agreement or contract between people.

Covenanters people who agree to a **covenant**.

deposed when a monarch is removed from the throne and no longer allowed to rule.

Dissenters members of religious groups not recognised as proper groups by the Church.

exile being sent away from your home town or country.

fire breaks obstacles used to try and stop the spread of a fire.

flogged beaten with a whip or a stick, as a punishment.

Gaelic the native language spoken in Ireland and Scotland.

grievances a list of complaints that have to be sorted out in Parliament.

guinea an old British gold coin, worth £1 and 1 shilling in old money. This was a large sum of money in Tudor and Stuart times.

intelligence work the collection of secret and important information for the government, usually done by government spies.

lobbying trying to persuade people in Parliament to support your views.

mutineers soldiers who rebel against their commanding officers and leaders.

outposts foreign branches of trading companies.

Papal Bull an order which comes directly from the Pope.

patron a person who gives money to support a group, like a theatre group.

peerages the rank in society of a nobleman.

pillory a wooden frame, with holes for the head and hands, which people were locked into as punishment.

pit the dug-out area in front of the stage, where people could stand to watch the play.

plantation land confiscated from the Irish by the English government, and given to Protestant people to live there.

Presbyterian a religion in which the Church is governed by elders, not bishops.

Privy Council a group of political advisors chosen by and for the monarch.

purged rid of people regarded as undesirable for whatever reason.

recusancy refusing to attend services of the Church of England, and attending Catholic services instead.

recusants people who are found guilty of **recusancy**.

Reformation the period in the sixteenth century when criticism of the Catholic Church led to the setting-up of Protestantism in parts of Europe.

republic a state in which power is held by the people or a group elected by them, and not by a monarch.

standard a distinctive flag or emblem, bearing the colours of a particular regiment.

succeeded be the next to rule after a monarch dies.

tuberculosis an infectious disease which attacks the lungs.

varicose veins veins, especially in the leg, which have become swollen and painful.

INDEX